WHAT THE POETS ARE DOING:

CANADIAN POETS IN CONVERSATION

WHAT THE POETS ARE DOING

CANADIAN POETS *in* CONVERSATION

Edited by

ROB TAYLOR

NIGHTWOOD EDITIONS
2018

Nightwood Editions
P.O. Box 1779
Gibsons, BC VON 1VO
Canada
www.nightwoodeditions.com

COVER DESIGN: Topshelf Creative
TYPOGRAPHY: Carleton Wilson

Canada

 Canada Council
for the Arts
Conseil des Arts
du Canada

 BRITISH COLUMBIA
ARTS COUNCIL
An agency of the Province of British Columbia

Nightwood Editions acknowledges the support of the Canada Council for the Arts, which last year invested $153 million to bring the arts to Canadians throughout the country. We also gratefully acknowledge financial support from the Government of Canada and from the Province of British Columbia through the BC Arts Council and the Book Publishing Tax Credit.

This book has been produced on 100% post-consumer recycled, ancient-forest-free paper, processed chlorine-free and printed with vegetable-based dyes.

Printed and bound in Canada.

CIP data available from Library and Archives Canada.

ISBN 978-0-88971-343-7

CONTENTS

WHAT THE POETS ARE DOING: A FOREWORD

This book exists because another one preceded it. Of course, every book could open with that note, but it's especially true here. If this book of conversations is in a conversation itself, it's with *Where the Words Come From*, published by Nightwood Editions in 2002 when I was nineteen years old and helplessly impressionable. In that book, up-and-coming Canadian poets interviewed their esteemed older colleagues: Atwood, Ondaatje, Page, Avison… the whole inaugural class of the CanLit Hall of Fame (don't laugh at the thought—I bet somewhere in York Mills or Kerrisdale a shipping magnate's elderly great-granddaughter is penning the seed funding into her will). I came across *Where the Words Come From* in a bookstore and brought it home. How could I not? I was already infatuated with poems—how reading them could reconfigure me—but I had yet to make the "choice" to become a poet. How does one even go about that? How can a poet *be*? I found, in that book, some answers. They were indirect, of course, accumulated more than understood. I remember the discussions of the "presentiment of loss" at the heart of Don Coles's poetry, the "imprint of the unsayable on what is said" in Jan Zwicky's and the "dance of simultaneous energies" and "rhythmic trek" in Dennis Lee's. The interviews in *Where the Words Come From* deepened my understanding of those poets, their craft and their lives in the art, enough to clear a path toward becoming a poet myself. No, that's not true. There's no damn path. But they hammered up a sign pointing into the jungle that said, "Oh, go for it." So I went.

Needless to say, *Where the Words Come From* was, and remains, one of my favourite books despite it having tricked me into what Chaucer should have called the "craft so disappointing to the in-laws." In preparing for a 2017 interview with *Where the Words Come From* editor Tim Bowling, I returned to the book and felt like I had been greeted by an old friend. A warmth generated by two poets reaching out to one another in shared curiosity still emanated from the book some fifteen years later, as I suspect it will for some time. "It's a shame there wasn't a sequel," I muttered to myself, thinking of all the years and poets and changes that have come in the interim. And then, with Tim's blessing and Silas White's willingness to embark on a doubtful commercial venture, we set about making a sequel happen.

The structure of this book mirrors the last, with a few key adjustments. We've added poems to the book—poems which, for the most part, are mentioned in the conversations themselves—in hopes they will deepen the reader's experience. We've also set out to have these be true *conversations* as opposed to interviews, with both poets posing questions to one another and contributing equally. Tied to that, while the book does adhere to the structure of pairing established and up-and-coming poets, the qualifications for who fits in which category were amorphous and largely ignored when finalizing a pairing. There are poets in the up-and-coming slots who have published as many books, or are nearly as old, as some of the "established" poets. Oh rule sticklers, it's a mess! Fortunately, you're entering a party and not a coronation.

Party guests in this project were invited directly from a list devised between Silas and me. I hoped a few of them might say *yes*. Nearly all of them did, with none balking at the idea of researching a younger partner as an equal (in fact, the only concerns about the structure were from established poets wishing to make sure they would in no way overshadow their partners). The established poets were then asked to select their partners; in some cases I recommended someone in particular, in others I presented a list of possibilities and in all cases I offered the chance for the poet to pick a partner of their own devising. All three paths were taken by one or more poets. Some selected poets were unable to participate for a variety of reasons. In other words, great thought went into these pairings, but that thought was decentralized and subject to the whims of time constraints and life events. The lineup changed many times. I developed—I'm sure time will prove out—a small ulcer, but I am thrilled with the group assembled here (which could have been many times larger as this country teems with talent, but that's an ulcer for another day).

All of the conversations in this book were conducted at some point between January and June of 2018. While *Where the Words Come From* featured a roughly fifty-fifty split between in-person and written interviews, almost all the conversations featured here were conducted online (the pros and cons of which are debated in Steven Heighton and Ben Ladouceur's conversation and returned to in Sue Sinclair and Nick Thran's afterword). Still, there is great variation in their nature. Some of the conversations developed slowly over four or five months, others were compressed into a matter of weeks. Some were written by steadily adding to a shared Word document (with its red and blue squiggly underlining nagging at each imperfection), while others were a series of email replies. Some were held between strangers and others between friends. All of this shifted the tone and diction, the confidence of questions and length of answers, in ways detectable and perhaps not.

As to the content, I encourage you to turn the page and find out for yourself. Or skip to the afterword for the Coles Notes—it's your book! All I'll say is that the poets in this book both challenged me and made me feel at home (in my language, my community, my self). They helped me reshape what that home looks and feels like, as they do in their poems. For that I am grateful to each one of them. And at the risk of sounding ridiculous to future readers (whenever anyone talks about the great literary feuds of the eighties and nineties I can only envision Casey and Finnegan squabbling over who gets to eat dessert first), I will add that the last few years have been a turbulent time for the Canadian writing community. Movements around sexual assault, racial discrimination, cultural appropriation, Indigenous-settler reconciliation, gender equality and more have resulted in seemingly equal parts progress and pushback with the responses of writers often split along generational lines. The old don't care about the young and the young are readying to devour the old, et cetera. There is some truth to that thinking, and a number of poets in this book confront its realities head on, but it's also a narrative that erases too many people and too much good and generous learning that is happening all the time across this supposedly great chasm. I hope that is made plain in the conversations here.

Four years before *Where the Words Come From* was published, The Tragically Hip released *Phantom Power* with its lead single, "Poets." The damn song was everywhere (the longest-reigning number one hit on the Canadian alternative charts). In its chorus, lead singer and lyricist Gord Downie (a published Canadian poet himself) admonishes the listener to stop telling him about tough-talking, anti-social poets who are also "somehow not anti-social enough." That chorus felt, for me, like an indictment and a challenge at once, hinging on two meanings of anti-social: "not sociable" and "contrary to the laws and customs of society." It's as though Downie were reminding us, *Hey artists, don't be too self-absorbed. There's work to be done out there in the world.* In hindsight, the song helped set the stage for the generations of poets to come, poets who reflect the diversity of perspectives and experiences in this country and who, in part because of that, are anti-social in all the right ways. We've made progress, but there's still work to be done, on the page and off, inside and out, poets and readers alike. So hell, Gord, we're going to tell you what the poets are doing. I think you'll be pleasantly surprised.

Rob Taylor
July 2018
Port Moody, BC

THE TOTAL MAMMAL:

Steven Heighton and Ben Ladouceur

Ben Ladouceur: To me, at first glance, the most interesting thing about your bibliography is how your relationship with poetry is marked by both commitment and infidelity. I think of the role models that I've been provided with as a poet. There are the poet-poets, whose books are all poetry, excepting maybe one or two forays into criticism or short fiction or some extremely autobiographical novel. There are also the traitors, who write a few poetry chapbooks or trade collections before they successfully pivot to some other written medium that's less cumbersome to explain to all the normal people at all the normal parties, and possibly more profitable too: fiction, film, theatre, music. Then there's you, alternating between poetry and fiction (and some non-fiction) with a consistency that's not often seen. I secretly want to do exactly this with my life. I want to write *everything*. But my poetry demands monogamy; when I venture into other written media, poetry gives me the cold shoulder. It threatens to leave me forever (although maybe it's all talk). I tell myself that this is an inevitable part of being a poet, but you single-handedly throw a wrench in my thesis with your weird, all-terrain career. What's your problem?

Steven Heighton: My waffling between genres actually *is* a problem in at least one way, which I'll describe below. So maybe you should choose genre-monogamy? If it is a choice. For me it wasn't. From the outset, creative impulses came to me either in narrative or in lyric form. There was no deliberate diversification; I wrote stories and poems (essays too) concurrently from the start. For whatever reason, I never saw poetry as inferior because of its minor word counts and modest cultural influence. I certainly never thought that writers, as they matured and grew "serious," should graduate to ever-larger and— as you put it—"possibly more profitable" forms.

So, my problem: over the last twenty years, because of how I've worked to develop a poet's sound sensitivities, at the level of the syllable, writing prose has become discouragingly arduous. At the moment I'm working on a ten-line poem that Kingston Parks and Rec has commissioned for the hockey boards of the outdoor rink in Skeleton Park, around the corner. (I like how "commission" suggests I'm being paid thousands to cast a bronze bust of a philanthropic patron.) I've done a number of drafts so far—mainly playing with the last three lines, varying the verbs and punctuation, trying to fine-tune the acoustics—and the project remains a pleasure. I don't and won't mind tinkering patiently to get it as right as I can. And here it lies, printed on my desk, a text-block the size of a playing card or canapé. It's still a challenge, but it's feasible. And if it fails and I have to walk away, big deal.

But then, to export this micropoetic focus, this criterion of intensity, to a prose work of a hundred thousand words… agony. And yet I feel I have no choice. The poet's internalized criterion, that standard of concision, clarity and euphony, is not something you can just dial down when you switch over to prose. There's no energy-saving "green" setting, at least not for me. And maybe that last phrase should give you hope, should you choose to cheat and write fiction. I mean, this "cursed with the poet's ear" stuff might sound like a veiled boast, but it's not. I do worry I'm wasting time being too fastidious. It *should* be possible for a prose stylist to revise less exhaustively and compulsively than a poet, at least in the more procedural parts of a book. Maybe my "criterion" is nothing but a clinical pathology, possibly a medicable one… On the other hand, if you're writing a short story, brace yourself. There's nowhere to hide. Every line has to be catechized and polished the way you polish a poem.

As for your feelings about poetry threatening to fire you for moonlighting, I've heard that some poets (Wallace Stevens and T.S. Eliot are examples from the past) find that working a "normal" full-time job actually sharpens their poetic practice because it confines and channels their energy and time. Maybe working in genres besides poetry could have that same effect for you. And here's a related metaphor: if you miss a night's sleep, and thus a night's worth of dreams, the next night you dream vividly and at great length as the expressive pressure of the nightmind finally finds release. So, in your case, maybe your instincts are whispering that you should avoid diffusing your energies but rather build and concentrate them, like dreams deferred on a sleepless night, or strong imagery bottled up during a workday.

Ladouceur: I too have a day job, one that has almost no content overlap with my creative life. I work at a small non-profit, coordinating and communicating. This set-up has been working out fine for me as a writer for a few reasons that I can detect, and probably yet other reasons I cannot detect. What's detectable: the change that is instigated by poetry and personal journalism can be, at best, very difficult to discern (or even to believe in), so it's been a nice counterbalance to work at an organization that's striving to make things better in the world in small and concrete ways. I also get to take the odd business trip, and the business trip is a really special category of time. Aside from the meetings you are travelling for, you spend a lot of time being lonely in a hotel room that has a desk and a window overlooking a city you do not live in. These are amazing conditions for creative productivity, rivalled perhaps only by the plane rides to and from, which are long, boring, antisocial and internet-free.

When I was twenty-five and I got my first few arts grants, I reduced my hours at Starbucks from forty hours per week to twenty hours per week. I thought *maybe I'll just live very affordably and make coffee sometimes and string together grants and freelance gigs until I die.* Then one night I woke up with a bone-crushing toothache. After a sleepless night of failed internet remedies, I sucked it up and spent over $100 on an emergency dentist appointment. One hundred dollars was a lot of money to me that year. At the appointment, I learned that the only way to stop the pain was a root canal that would cost over $2500. I thanked the dentist and paid the receptionist and went to the building stairwell and cried and cried. I ate the painkillers they gave me and watched *9 to 5* with a dear friend. I resolved to get a job, something with benefits, somewhere, somehow, down the line: a nine to five. It was all very formative.

Many remarkable writers and artists tolerate or even derive creative energy from the nibbling fear of where future money will come from. I found it too stressful. There were fewer ideas, fewer poems, instead of more. My big point is that having a day job has been artistically enabling to me. It takes care of the money so I can rest easy and write the things I find fun and personally important. Even if I didn't have to work, and I had every hour of my day to dedicate to writing, I'm not convinced I'd write that much more than I do now. When I was at the Al Purdy A-Frame for three months with a monthly stipend and a rental car and often no company, I got a lot done at first, but before long my productivity wound down. I also felt painfully guilty on days the writing went

STEVEN HEIGHTON AND BEN LADOUCEUR

poorly. When I confessed all of this to Al's widow Eurithe during one of her visits to the house, she mentioned your name; apparently you told her that three months is just too long for a residency. What experience made you share this with her?

Heighton: I did tell Eurithe that I thought three months was too long. My longest residency experience was two months, down at the Wurlitzer Foundation retreat in Taos, New Mexico, back in 1998. I loved the adobe casita they installed me in, I loved the combined hippy/redneck vibe of the town, I loved the desert and the mountains and did plenty of running and walking there. I also wrote 250 pages of prose—a raw draft of the middle section of my first novel, *The Shadow Boxer*. It was mostly self-indulgent and verbose. I realized after the fact that I'd simply had too much freedom, too much time. Is that really possible? I discovered it was. I had no email back then and of course the Internet was not the dopamine dispenser and time vortex it is now. Nowhere close. So I sat and wrote six to eight hours a day. I felt drunk with the exhilaration of it. Page after page, it flowed out with easy fluency and a (spurious) sense of freshness and rightness. But as Duke Ellington said, "It's good to have limits." I needed a more pressing schedule, to enforce discipline, to cinch in that loquacity, to make me prioritize and triage. I mean, there's a fine line here; in a first draft you want to grant yourself leeway to digress, meander, take risks and blow it, but even in a first draft you need some constraints, some pressure. Thinking you have all the time in the world is probably not healthy. I feel now that two to four weeks would be ideal, at least for me.

Work that comes easily and quickly can of course be good. That's what Salvador Dali seems to be getting at with his dictum, "It's either easy or it's impossible." My Skeleton Park poem was supposed to have something to do with skating; I love skating and hockey and have always wanted to write a poem that sonically embodies the movement and sounds of skating. So I sat down to write and the ten-line poem came in minutes. I've revised certain lines repeatedly, as I said, but the poem's basic arc, its argument, has been there from the start. As if the poem was already internally crystallized and waiting to be discovered—a rare feeling but one that I think most poets sometimes experience. Actually, a better metaphor might involve a cook's *mise en place*. Everything needed to produce the finished dish is out on the counter; the cook enters the kitchen and puts it together.

Ladouceur: How much are you getting paid for your Skeleton Park poem?

Heighton: Nobody seems to know! Ever get the feeling that poets are expected not to bring up money—as if the world is doing them a favour by inviting them to read their work or write something new? As if we're being humoured as much as honoured (as in the term "honorarium")?

Maybe they should pay us a humorarium.

Two questions for you: Is Dali right in the sense that difficult poems—willed poems, poems strenuously constructed against some kind of perceived semantic or conceptual resistance—are missing some essential factor that's present in "discovered" poems? My other question stems from my sense that I can spot a poem that bushwhacked the poet and came quickly. "Salutations from Abitibi" is one of many strong poems in your first full collection, *Otter*. Is it also one that came quickly, easily, organically (which, by the way, is a word I vowed I would not use in this conversation, along with "curate")?

SALUTATIONS FROM ABITIBI
Ben Ladouceur

Alone clouds refused to cohere.
They darkened the city in blotches.
They rendered the city dalmatian.

I forgot my lover on the bus.
The brakes woke him up
at Abitibi and he found work there.

All year mosquitoes bit his fumbling frame.
The bites were like Grecian constellations
seen on a clear taupe day.

My Zippo was on his person.
I was planning to quit with the smoking
but how shall I now singe the frays

STEVEN HEIGHTON AND BEN LADOUCEUR

of my only warm coat? When winter arrives
the mosquitoes will expire
and material will cover the bodies of men.

At least I received a blank postcard
on the birthday of my lover.
Its message: *I am alive I am alone*

I am not willing to speak. Some men
are darkened in the long run, by sun.
Others, more quickly, by clouds.

Ladouceur: Yep, that's accurate, that was a single-sitting poem. I knew it was going to be book-good less than halfway through writing it, so I borrowed chunks from less successful poems in my drafts folders and made a nice little Frankenstein out of darlings. I'm glad you like that poem. It's so funny what poems are found strong by whom. There are poems and lines in *Otter* that people cite as favourites but that I don't even remember the entire genesis of and feel no heightened pride toward. There are also parts which I consider my beautiful, little, golden children born to amaze civilizations present and future but which have elicited zero response to date. One of the lessons I learned while publishing *Otter* was that there's very little correlation between the poems that are important to me and the poems that are important to a given readership. You can make the poems good but you can't control whether they are dear to anyone. Is that fair to say?

In any case, I've refined my approach to poetry in the past few years if only to ensure the next book doesn't move like a B-side to *Otter*. I used to write shitloads of poems and see what was good, how sea invertebrates lay a zillion eggs and hope that a handful survive. Now I'm a lot less prolific, on purpose, and a lot more attentive to each creation—a total mammal. One fun side effect of this change is that I expect more from the poems, not in terms of how well they entertain, but in terms of how well they tell the truth. I want them to praise the things I love, or to lament the things I suffer from or both and vice-versa.

What kind of animal are you, with your poems? I have no inkling with your work. I'd say they seem well-incubated and fully developed, but octopuses seem that way too. Are thousands of failures buried out back?

Heighton: Most of the buried failures are from years ago when my poetic reproductive strategy—great metaphor—was less mammalian. These days I write far fewer poems, partly because I now have to devote most of my writing time to other genres, but also because I've gotten better at recognizing authentic, worthwhile impulses when they wake me at night. And it occurs to me now: if I tallied up the number of *real* poems I've written per year over the past thirty years, the rate has likely stayed steady (and very low), even though for the last ten years I've started far fewer poems than I used to. Which raises an interesting possibility: that as poets we receive authentic poems at a certain limited rate and we can't force that rate higher—can't force real poems into being.

Your praise/lament line seems to sample one of my epigraphs from *The Waking Comes Late*: "Nor shall I care to write poetry that is not praise, lamentation, or both." The epigraph and its long-deceased author, Stamatis Smyrlis, are invented, naturally. But I digress. I meant to say that I'm pleased you agree that celebration and elegy remain embraceable poetic principles. I don't see the point of writing poems otherwise. I used to worry that I'd sound obsolete or nostalgic for saying such things, even from behind the death-mask of a nonexistent Greek poet. I couldn't care less now.

Speaking of caring less, or more: many poetry collections these days receive few if any reviews, sadly. I know *Otter* did receive attention, but instead of asking you how you felt about the reviews I want to know what an ideal assessment of one of your books would look like. Would it be gratifyingly, entirely glowing? Would it be conflicted, maybe even exasperated at times? If so, would the reservations out your own secret reservations about your writing or completely blindside you and suggest problems you never suspected?

Ladouceur: My ideal reader is an individual, as in, a single human. If I have one person in mind as I write, probably a person near to the heart, I wind up with this blood-lined sort of verisimilitude that others, even strangers, can still find interesting and entertaining. But sharing my work with strangers (also known as publishing) is important to me too, so I try to avoid letting intimate content become esoteric content. This takes doing. Some of my favourite poems of mine (though none of my best) will always be fully legible to one person only.

Any assessment about the work is an ideal assessment; reviews and responses are rare to come by in the first place, as you say. If a review is glowing, it's so lovely and warm to the touch. I'll feel that little glow in my chest all day, even though my writing probably won't benefit in any significant way. Positive reinforcement has its place, especially with new poets, but at this point in my life I will keep writing all my feelings down no matter what. If the review is critical, or even negative, and the reviewer's route to that conclusion is plausible to me, then I'll be happy to learn something true and new. (*Ideally*, I mean. In addition to an ideal reader, there's an ideal *self* involved in the poem too. That's the guy who accepts critical feedback happily. In reality, for a time it just smarts and the gratitude comes way later.)

On the other hand, some reviews seem to come from malice, and who would feel gratitude for that? In the worlds of poetry and independent publishing, I'm skeptical of the utility of strongly negative reviews. If you dislike a book and believe that other human beings are better off not reading it, then probably the most effective thing you can do is not write a review. Maybe negative reviews of "big-name" poets' works are more justified in that a lot of light is already shed on their work and people might already be thinking about investing time and money in the book, but if you're dedicating precious review space to tearing a poetry collection apart, you have to do an exceptionally good job of scaring readers away from the text in question. Bad-bad reviews (as in, reviews that are both negative and poorly written) make me buy the book. I become curious; I want to go see what got someone so passionate. I've yet to receive this kind of scorching review—maybe that will come with book number two.

Is there anything that more than one reviewer/reader has misunderstood, to your mind, about any or all of your work? Any advice for how authors can cope when this happens?

Heighton: Carmine Starnino and I once argued about scathing reviews. I said pretty much the same as you—given that there's so little reviewing space, why not just ignore books we don't like and devote any available opportunities to endorsing whatever we feel people should be reading? Speak up for what we love and otherwise leave the triage to time. Carmine's counter-argument—I believe I'm quoting him accurately—was that "posterity starts now." He felt strongly that if we didn't intervene in that triage, specious work might prevail, at least temporarily. It's a plausible position, and Carmine did put his money where his mouth was—he uncomplainingly absorbed as many shots as he gave—but in the end I kept my opinion.

That was ten years ago. Now, with so many folks indulging in online ire-gasms, solo or in cybermobs, the last thing we need is more public cruelty, more scorn and shaming. It is possible to criticize honestly and intelligently without being cruel. It's harder work, but it's possible. A recent review of my poetry contained some negative criticism. I loved the review, even if I didn't agree with the critique. It was collegial, it was human-to-human. We're in the midst of a terrifying partisanization of the culture—both aesthetic and political—and maybe one way to intervene in the crisis is through small gestures of respect.

THE LAST STURGEON
Steven Heighton

Deltawave shadows
of his deeds
and didn'ts, slid
under his shoes
like fillet knives, severing
soles from soil,
so he always walked
a little above his life,
not knowing it was
his life, while it waned
from waking-coma
to coma.
      Came a land-
locked night
he dreamed that he'd

landed the last sturgeon in the world
and she looked bad—
shrunken, bludgeoned,
a blue-ribbed CAT scan
of herself, her buckled
gills gawping,
a foam of green roe
welling from her mouth.

Each egg
was a tear, a tiny, entreating
vowel he couldn't quite hear
as he cast round the boat (now morphing
into a mountain shack)
for *water*, the merest
rainpool, he panicked,
or glacial stream,
my dearest,
my loved one,
let me bear you back
to haven—by river
the ocean
is never far.

Ladouceur: Probably! Probably gestures of respect would help. And human-to-human behaviour. I've been fortunate to meet a lot of poets I adore in the flesh and the friendships that spring from that are like nothing else. In the flesh there's no baggage, no pretense, no time to find the perfect thing to say. You just say the thing and it's the honest thing; it came from you unfiltered. Given too much time, words can get mean, moralistic, mildewy. There's nothing like an in-person conversation to collaboratively locate the truth with somebody. (Tangential comment: these in-the-flesh poets do not pop out of my drawers when I dress for work, nor do they materialize at the foot of my bed when I wake in the night. You know how I've been able to meet so many poets in the years before and since my book came out? Events. Events! Festivals, reading series, house readings, book launches, fundraisers, open mics. I love events. The noblest people in literature today might be the people who organize in-person literary events.)

Even the conversation we're currently having is a bit silly to me because it isn't happening in person or over the phone; we are emailing a Word document to each other, back and forth. Sometimes I change the phrasing on an answer I have had literal months to consider. I even have the option of re-phrasing my question following the advent of your response so that we both sound smarter! In my capacity as Prose Editor for *Arc*, I have asked a few poets if they'd be interested in phone interviews rather than the now-standard email interview. I have only been met with resistance on this front from both emerging and established authors. I get that, but upon publication I always take the measure to clarify—as I am also clarifying right now—that these interviews are not live, are not *alive*, are not from mouths in motion. These are the words of slow fingers and this birthing method imparts a different quality to the content. I think now of food photography, how it's easier to use plastic lettuce and spray-polished patties than to use real food. Of course it's easier and prettier, but is it the thing to do? I think now also of *Stalin's Architects*, your first book which was reissued a few years ago. In the foreword you admit to editing the book a little, as you also did with some reissued fiction of yours. How did it feel to do this? Amongst the feelings this activity provoked, could you detect any dishonesty, for instance?

Heighton: I think I prefer your version of my title to the actual one, *Stalin's Carnival*. And in the spirit of your remarks here, I'm going to insist that we stet it.

I agree that spontaneous remarks can be honest, but they're not always clear, hence my resistance to interviews transcribed straight from conversation. What use is honesty if readers miss the point of what I'm trying to say? For me, revision in a back and forth interview like this one serves the same purpose as gradual, careful revisions in fiction or poetry: trying to get my words and thoughts right and clear, rather than leaving that labour to the reader. I feel I should be cleaning up my own spills and I make a lot of them. It's possible you don't, so that a live interview would work better for you. I know several writers who speak in neat, coherent paragraphs (which are still full of vitality—clarity doesn't have to be dull and studied).

But the problem, for me, goes deeper than clarity. What I say off the cuff is not only unclear but sometimes *not what I actually think* because often I don't yet know what I think and I won't know until I start talking about it or writing about it, rambling a little, circumambulating an idea/meaning that I can't quite see, then circling, fumbling, groping inward, closer and closer. So for me revision isn't about falsifying my ideas but rather *finding* them, then presenting them to a reader in a form that skips those parts of my fumbling process that would seem too long, slow or repetitive, et cetera. But is something squandered in the process, some kind of first-draft vitality? Probably. Maybe it comes down to the difference between speech and writing. If I saw a writer being interviewed live on stage and reading an answer from prepared notes, I'd be disappointed. I want and expect a live interview to involve improv—jazz-like conceptual riffs, small gaffes, sheepish retractions, bold statements that seem to strike the speakers themselves as spontaneous discoveries. Beautiful. Private conversations can and should have that same quality of solo or mutual discovery. But that's spoken language. Written language is deeply different. Right now you and I can't rely on facial cues, body language or gestures, not to mention assenting nods or requests for clarification to help us land our meanings. In revising we can deploy typographic and orthographic versions of those clarifying cues—italics for emphasis, say, or punctuation as a kind of orthographic stand-in for hand gestures. Em dashes can work that way—I use them here and there to slow things down, to set off a qualification in the same way I might raise both hands in conversation to frame a parenthetical idea. And maybe this takes us back to those online iregasms. It seems clear that the escalatory vitriol of online exchanges has a lot to do with folks keyboarding too fast and failing to convey nuances—and truth is in the nuances, right? Also, the shorter the statement—280 characters for instance—the *more* time and effort it'll take to make a meaning clear.

As for *Stalin's Architects* (stet) and my first two story collections, when I began preparing the revised editions I made a deal with myself: I could make small fixes like changing words that seemed plainly wrong or deleting idle adverbs and unnecessary or inaccurate adjectives (once I substituted the correct "trowel" for the wordy, imprecise and weirdly brain-dead "small hand shovel"). In the poems, for acoustical or semantic reasons, I sometimes prodded punctuation and nudged line breaks but I disqualified myself from making changes that violated the character or spirit of any poem or story. I'd been a different person when I wrote the originals. If I now superimposed the tastes of a forty- or fifty-year-old on stories and poems written by someone in his late twenties, I might create a monstrous hybrid and also lose a precious vitality. Youth should have its say, and it only gets one chance. If I found the spirit of a story or poem too immature, I'd have to cut it—and that's what I did in the case of one story and four poems. As for whether any of that activity was aesthetically dishonest, it's for others to judge. I don't think so myself. If I'd known in 1990—as I should have known—more of the specific vocab of manual labour, I would have given that small hand shovel its proper name. Trowel. Beautiful word.

I'm saying I think it's okay to fix mistakes that don't alter your vision. And, yes, I did just go back through this answer and fix some gaffes and clean up a few spills—but I did it fast and just once. So, *stet*. Next time instead, we'll talk in person.

OUR BOREAL ROOTS:

Armand Garnet Ruffo and Liz Howard

Liz Howard: As a way of beginning I want to acknowledge our shared connection of place. We both grew up in the small town of Chapleau, Ontario, a former fur-trading outpost tucked just inside the arctic watershed. It is a very complicated place: geographically isolated with anglophone, francophone and First Nations communities, and also an often-ignored residential school past. It always seemed to me a pretty unlikely place to have produced a poet, let alone two. I want to tell the story of how I'm pretty sure I first came across your work, again in such an unlikely place: on the Toronto subway. At the time I was a psychology student and had been writing poetry in secret for years and one day on my way to class I saw a poem in place of what would have been an ad in the subway car I was riding.

THE FALLOUT
Armand Garnet Ruffo

I never asked my auntie what she learned
in Residential School. What comes to mind
is her beading and sewing, the moccasins
she made for us, the precision.

What I don't recall are any hugs or kisses
like my European relatives lavished on us.
As though the heirs of Columbus has a special
claim to affection for those like us
caught in between.

Even more surprising was the bio beneath it that told me the poem was written by an Armand Garnet Ruffo, a poet of Ojibwe descent originally from Chapleau, Ontario. I was absolutely stunned. I of course immediately looked up your work after class and was thrilled to get to finally meet you years later.

I tell this story by way of opening up a conversation around how our poetics are tied to place and the different ways we have used them to explore complicated identity. For example, in this poem that appeared on the TTC, taken from your book *At Geronimo's Grave* (Coteau Books, 2001), you speak directly of family members on both sides of your family, European and First Nations, and reference that your auntie attended residential school. In my own writing, my First Nations heritage always emerged as a troubled, occluded, coded presence very much as it was in life as I was estranged from that side of my family. Did you always write about family and/or "identity," "Nativeness" or "mixedness" in poetry? Is it something that always came through your work, something you sought to explore through the medium, or was it something that was born out of your poetic practice itself? Can you talk about how the medium and subject came about for you and how it has evolved?

Armand Garnet Ruffo: First I need to say that I'm equally thrilled to meet another poet from Chapleau—an award-winning one at that. I suppose the best way to begin is to point out that we are a generation apart. To put it another way, I could be your father. I say this because growing up in the sixties and coming of age in the seventies, there were still a lot of Indigenous people around who spoke their language and literally lived in the bush. For example, when I was about twelve I started working for a Cree outfitter who hosted American tourists at the camps he had built on a few lakes near Chapleau. All the other guides who worked for him were older than me, and though some of them likely went to the St. John's Residential School in Chapleau and experienced trauma (nobody talked about it), to me they seemed secure in their identities. And since I was at an impressionable age, this experience had a profound effect on me. I also need to point out that my own grandmother spoke Ojibwemowin as did my mother, though not as fluently. My grandmother—Wawatasie—was also our family historian, and the one who told me about our family and Grey Owl in and around Biscotasing, hence my book about him. And, of course, I can't forget my auntie who made us new moccasins every year. Although I didn't have an intimate relationship with my white father, what I can say about him is that he began his working life as a bush guide, and later got a job on the CPR when he started to raise a family (not with my mother). To give you a sense of the times, he was raised in Mettagama, a village that doesn't even exist any longer, and started working on steam engines! When I look back on my early years, it is clear to me that the land—the boreal forest, hunting, fishing and guiding—was all central to my life and shaped who I am today.

As for poetry itself, in my formative years in Chapleau, I didn't have any Indigenous literary models as there were precious few Indigenous writers getting published at the time. In fact, the only living poet I knew was Leonard Cohen because my sister had gone south to study nursing and brought back his first album, *Songs of Leonard Cohen*, which eventually led me to his books. Aside from him, my models were singer-songwriters like Johnny Cash, Gordon Lightfoot and Bob Dylan. When I started writing a little in high school, I naturally gravitated to their work. Then in the seventies I attended York University, and one weekend I went to visit my grandmother who was living with an aunt in Toronto. I can't recall exactly how it happened, but my grandmother and I started to talk about poetry—maybe she asked me about my classes— and she recited some of her poetry to me. Yes, recited! While her poems were very much in the style of Pauline Johnson, a form that I couldn't appreciate, I was blown away by the content. I still recall one of her poems, which begins with "Lost am I in my Native Land." Something clicked, and from that moment I had my material: I started to write about my life in the north and explored my Indigenous roots, which led to my first book, *Opening in the Sky*, the title coming from the English translation of my great-great-grandfather's name.

As for the specific poem you saw on the Toronto subway, one thing I remember about my grandmother and aunties is how little physical contact there was between us. Certainly they showed their affection in other ways like making me moccasins, but for whatever reason—sociologists, among others, now trace it to residential school and colonization—they rarely expressed emotion. This was very different from my father's family. I guess the poem arises then from both experience and observation. In referring to the heirs of Columbus, I'm referencing my European relatives and of course the claiming of the land and colonization in general.

As for how my subject matter has "evolved," I think it's become more expansive and complicated as I've experienced more and have come under various artistic and personal influences. That said, I think the themes have remained much the same. I'm still writing about colonization and its repercussions, identity, relationships, nature, language, et cetera, but it's how I'm saying these things that continues to evolve. I'm thinking of *The Thunderbird Poems*, which includes elements of Ojibwe ontology—spirituality, the mythic. When I was in my twenties, Wilfred Peltier, an Odawa "wiseman"—he didn't use the term elder—told me that you cannot be half of anything. Even if you are mixed blood, uprooted or whatever, you have to be a whole human being and I suppose that's what I've strived to be, both in my writing and in my life. I think one of the things people need to realize is that in Indigenous culture—at least in Ojibwe—it is the women who pass on culture to the children, especially in the early years, and I happened to grow up with some strong Ojibwe women (Anishinaabekwe), meaning that they survived against incredible odds and so I guess that's where my writing (mostly) comes from.

Howard: I think it is crucial to point out as you have that we are a generation apart because I feel, or at least I've come to know it to be the case in my own experience, that so much can happen in one generation, especially since our work is connected in its drawing upon this tension between a so-called "dominant" culture and one that is under the threat of erasure or assimilation. Within a generation so much can be lost. It is so moving for me to hear you speak of growing up with these Indigenous role models: in the outfitter men you worked for and also your own grandmother who spoke the language. It has always been a source of sadness and difficulty for me (but also a part of my own journey of discovering who I am and who my relations are) that I was completely estranged from my father's side of the family (it is his mother's family that I have my most direct Ojibwe ancestry). She spoke the language and was raised in the culture. Her mother and father came from Atikameksheng Anishnawbek (formerly Whitefish Lake First Nation) just outside of Sudbury, Ontario. My father unfortunately suffered badly from substance abuse issues and was actually a missing person for years.

As an aside, I almost started crying when you said (just as fact of age difference, I know) that you could be my father. I just got back from this whirlwind Maritime tour. I spent the first night in Halifax during an intense nor'easter. My father ended up in Halifax at the end of his life as a bottle picker. He surfaced when his liver started failing and had to reach out to family to get documents for a health card. My aunt eventually reached out to me when he was dying and I flew out there in January of 2015. I think he held on for me because he only lasted about twenty minutes after I arrived at the hospital. That was the first and last time I ever met him. I was stuck there a week in storms helping my aunt arrange things afterward. It was so strange because technically I was next of kin so was asked all the questions (what prayers at the funeral, where to cast ashes, et cetera) but had never met the man. His partner eventually gave me his effects, papers and the like, that told his story. He'd tried to get help, get clean. He had pictures of me and family payment statements he'd kept pristine. He just couldn't shake drinking and it killed him at fifty-one.

When I started writing emotionally propulsive poetry as a young person I found myself addressing my father, my grandmother, my ancestors. Somehow it was a natural conduit for me. When I moved to the city I used to study the faces of every man begging on the street to see if I could recognize something of myself in him, to see if he was my father. It wasn't until years later through my own research that I learned about the sacred rite of the shaking tent. How it was used as a vehicle of prophesy or communication at a distance. I realized I had been using poetry in the same way. To try and reach my father, my relatives.

Have you ever had an experience of the sacred in your writing? Or perhaps you can talk about writing through the shamanic works of Norval Morrisseau and not only writing a biography about him but also writing poems in response to his paintings?

Ruffo: Sorry for making you cry. What I find interesting is how much our poetry is linked, whether directly or indirectly, to our Indigenous heritage and our connection to place. In other words, we cannot talk about our work separated from our life experience. I was recently reading about Elizabeth Bishop and learned that she drank heavily all her life and had been separated from her Nova Scotian grandparents, whom she apparently loved dearly, at an early age. I'm mentioning this because from her poetry you would never know it. And yet while she was writing her observational kind of poetry, a whole school of confessional style poetry came into prominence. In fact, Robert Lowell, one of the foremost proponents of confessional poetry, was a friend of Bishop's. There we have it, the impact of the confessional and yet the urge to do something else: to move either behind language or deep into the mechanics of it. This is something that Indigenous poets are not immune to. For example, would I be wrong to say that in *Infinite Citizen of the Shaking Tent* you bury—is that the correct word?—much of what you said about your father and your relationship to your mixed heritage within a kind of labyrinthine language fixed in science? In contrast to direct confessional poetry, there's usually something else going on in your work that deviates from stating things directly. A poem like "Thinktent" comes to mind. There's just so many references moving tangentially outward from direct familial-Indigenous experience.

While you mention that you were using the poetry in that collection to try and reach your father, I wonder if you were actually writing *for* your father. It seems to me the kind of poetic incantation you conceptualize is extremely personal in its concern for language and Western epistemology. That those Canadian poets who foreground linguistic and textual process over content, language over experience, received your book so enthusiastically speaks volumes about the tension that exists in contemporary poetry. Like I said, this tension also exists in the work of Indigenous poets, more so now than ever before, but because of our political reality it's just not as pervasive. In fact, it seems to me the Indigenous poets concerned about this kind of thing try to combine these disparate strands. The poets working with Indigenous languages come to mind here. I would go so far as to say that the scientific language you choose intentionally complicates direct experience probably because the experiences you write about are so painful for you, and because you find yourself "outside of the shaking tent looking in." Is that a fair assessment?

There are a couple of poems in the collection, like "Look Book," that are more directly engaged with experience, but I think they are the exception. In "Knausgaard, Nova Scotia," however, the poem you published in *Dusie*, there's no misunderstanding in the fourth stanza:

EXCERPT FROM "KNAUSGAARD, NOVA SCOTIA"
Liz Howard

My father's skin had yellowed and the sclerae of his eyes,
half open but clouded by sedation. A tear slid
from the corner of his right eye to past the bone
of his indigenous cheek. This tear had not yet dried
when they began to withdraw life support, machine
by machine. The breathing machine that jerked his
head back and expanded his chest with decreasing

regularity was the last to be withdrawn. A nurse said,
"He is in the process of actively dying now."
Actively dying.

As for my biography *Norval Morrisseau: Man Changing into Thunderbird*, I in-
itially assumed it would be completely prose, but as I got into his life and art,
I found that poems started to appear and I just let them come. A tap had been
opened and the few poems in the biography grew into a book of their own,
The Thunderbird Poems. I realized in the process that poetry can handle things
that prose can't, or at least poetry can do it much more succinctly. It was then
that I started to think of the form of the poetry I was writing, and I knew that I
wanted it to engage with a particular kind of experience; it had to be grounded
in the world of the Anishinaabek Manidoog or Manitous.

I was concerned about employing the world of shamanism in the work
because that was Norval's world and he always said that his paintings came
directly out of it. (Norval's grandfather, Potan Nanakonagos, was a shaman
and his greatest influence.) I was also leaning toward direct confession because
Norval himself had told me "not to leave anything out." Furthermore, because
Norval believed his art had the power to guide Indigenous people back to our
traditions, I wanted Indigenous people to be the first audience, above all, to
identify with the work. So while the tension between observation and confes-
sion is there, the majority of the poems are grounded in narrative, which serves
to anchor them in a particular Anishinaabek experience and meaning. Take
my poem "Ancestors Performing the Ritual of the Shaking Tent, c. 1958–61"
which strives to bring the reader into the actual process of the ceremony—as
Norval's artwork elicits—as opposed to conceptualizing the ritual in a wider
application and extrapolating upon it. I might add that there are fifty-three
poems in the book and I thought I would make it an even sixty. Easier said than
done. I went to galleries, read art books about him, went for walks, but nothing
came. The poetry had come quickly and it had left just as quickly.

All this makes me wonder about the responsibility and the role of poets,
Indigenous poets in particular. Can we as literary artists do our own thing
above all else or are we compelled by our histories and reality as colonized
peoples? To paraphrase Laguna Pueblo writer Paula Gunn Allen, there's no
cavalry riding over the hill to come to our rescue, to be spokespeople for our
communities. The living and the dead. To put this another way, are we writ-

ing for the children who were beaten and starved to death in the residential schools? I'm thinking here of the tiny graves hidden in the bush near the old St. John's Residential School in Chapleau. Is writing as artists with no responsibility but to ourselves and our art a luxury we can afford?

Howard: Your response is sending me off into so many possible nodes that I want to explore and that I feel are all equally necessary, valid and interesting, and that is exactly the point, really, of the concatenating, transgressive, paradoxical excess you speak of in my work. What can come off as a burying, concealment, occlusion, is really an attempt to render on the page what is happening in my mind. My ultimate confession, as you have got so right, is a disaster of language as a result of trauma. There is the fear of revealing too much. There is the fear of not getting it right. There is the fear of it not really being my right to speak, even if it is my own experience. The poems in *Infinite Citizen of the Shaking Tent* were for the most part composed in 2010–2014 and during that time what I knew of my Indigenous heritage was conveyed to me by my mother, who I love and respect dearly, but who has suffered from mental health issues and has therefore been very much the unreliable narrator of my life. Growing up as I did (experiencing abuse as a young adult while writing and also working through depression, anxiety, PTSD as well as substance issues), there was very much for me an issue of not trusting my own mind, my own narrative and my own stories enough to tell them "straight." When I was writing my book the chaos I was feeling in my mind, my soul and my emotions came through in the language I was using. Just as the land is contaminated by industry, so too, in a way, is my own "story" "contaminated" by Western ideology, right? All these complications are pulled through the book. If you read and reread the book you will see the larger themes start to come into relief, stories pop out. I think my future work will be largely more "accessible" in style. But I loved experimenting in this way. It felt true to me. To how I was feeling at the time. There was, as you said, a sense of being outside the tent. But I also identified with the figure of Mikanaak (or Mikkinnuk as you write it in *The Thunderbird Poems*), the turtle spirit in the tent. The one who receives Manidoog knowledge in their disparate languages and translates them into Anishinaabemowin for the conjuror of the tent rite, as I came to understand it in my research. Sometimes one doesn't always get the translation right, you know what I mean? When I was allowing myself to attune to the paradoxical linguistic crosscurrents in my mind I caught and translated onto the page what I found there. Sometimes it was a story from my childhood I felt brave enough to share. Sometimes it was a bit of the Ojibway language I taught myself, a reference to a Nanabush story or a memory of being blessed by an elder in Chapleau. Other times it was an anatomical term or philosophical theory I learned in university, big words I learned in books, stories I heard of the things people did to hurt each other or to help each other, things that made me laugh. All of it toward a kind of prophesy, a question I asked myself: Am I worth it to continue? Are my people out there? Am I alone in this?

Of course everything was different when I wrote the elegy for my father. That was after I met him for the first and last time. That was the answer to the big question. Seeing my father, there was no question what my ancestry was, although I know it's not the same as having a community that recognizes you. But I met my aunty too and she told me the family story. A veil was lifted. In grief there is just the force of the immediate over and over and over. And I think that's what comes through in my poem. It's been the most impactful thing I've written. It's the thing that scared me the most to share because it's so close to me. So I've become more open to writing in this way. It still scares me. I truly think there's room for both ways, the chaos and the personal. That's what I identify with.

And so as you have said in writing about Norval and his life and work and referencing in particular his painting "Ancestors Performing the Ritual of the Shaking Tent, c. 1958-61" and his shaman grandfather, you must know the story. The story I'm thinking of is the one he's told of witnessing the Shaking Tent in a neighbour's house because it was outlawed at the time. Practitioners were actually imprisoned if caught. So it was being done in a house and he recounts how he couldn't believe it. When I read Norval's account I had such a feeling in my chest. This is the strange horror of assimilation that I know. What is a room? A cell? A containment? A collection of lines in poetry is called a stanza. Stanza means room in Italian. Poetry is often about compression. What of this moment of secreting away an oracular practice? My ancestors did this too in the open. I never will. What do I accomplish in my little rooms of chaos? As you have asked, what is the larger responsibility?

Ruffo: What immediately comes to my mind from your response is a history of silence and lies that is the foundation upon which this country is built—

meaning a history of racism, violence and displacement—and this is the foundation upon which Canadians have built their homes (and families). Generations of Indigenous people, including members of both our families, have lived and died tragically, and for us it's the norm! On the literary front, these experiences are finally being documented. As I said earlier, when I started writing I was hard-pressed to find a role model. Today, any aspiring Indigenous writer only has to walk into a library or bookstore and there's a shelf of Indigenous writers. That's nothing less than amazing. I think a large part of it has to do with what you are getting at. In the past we tended to conceal and sublimate our Indigenous identities just as the colonizer wanted and expected us to do. I remember my mother telling me that when she was young she and a friend went to Toronto and worked as waitresses in a restaurant. My mother passed herself off as Spanish and her girlfriend passed herself off as Asian. Had they said they were "Indian" they wouldn't have gotten the jobs. At the time my mother told me this I was fairly young and I didn't realize the pain that must have surfaced for her in telling me. That's what we went through, a whole people! Most Canadians don't want to know this stuff. Reconciliation to them is something *out there*, something intangible that really has nothing to do with them. "It happened before I was born." We hear that a lot. But who benefitted? So, yes, something positive is currently happening in the country and I'm happy to be alive to witness it.

To complicate matters, is the notion of "responsibility" leading to a circumscription of what Indigenous poetry, and Indigenous literature in general, is supposed to be? There currently seems to be a trend to emphasize the aforementioned traumas I was talking about with little consideration given to the positive aspects of having Indigenous heritage. And what about aesthetics? It is as though Indigenous people never had an interest in such questions, when one only has to turn to our traditional storytelling strategies or our sense of design, our totems or basketry, to see the truth. Take the current field of Indigenous literary studies; it seems to be almost solely focused on a literature of trauma and resistance. I guess what I'm getting at: Is our literature at risk of becoming a literature of issues? While you refer to your book *Infinite Citizen* as "a disaster of language" with all kinds of "complications… pulled through the book," it nevertheless employs language in inventive ways to explore another potential aesthetic for Indigenous poets. In this way, one could consider your text as providing an alternative to this circumscription, this pigeonholing.

I'm also thinking here of other young Indigenous writers who are pushing the aesthetic button while dealing with their own issues—yikes, there's that word again.

Howard: I think you're exactly right that there is this all-too-steady gaze on the traumatic Indigenous experience. I also often wonder about what might be called Indigenous "futurisms," or futures or possibilities, aesthetic potentials as you have said. I think I have made a way toward that in my work. At least that was the intention, the necessity. The fracturing, the hardship, the wound, whether within oneself and/or within one's lineage as an Indigenous person is a fact. The question is, what to do? Ultimately for myself as a writer, I discovered the figure of the infinite citizen of the shaking tent. Perhaps I am a kind of slippery, in-between, trickster spirit. I suppose this is the figure of myself as a writer that could compose in so many formally inventive and generative ways, pulling in neuroscience, the bush, Western philosophy, Nanabozho, dreams, calling down the sky, Toronto streets, ecological concerns and so on, and compressing them all together into my account, my gift, my book. The trauma, the silence, the absence is there too. But I think it is an ultimately joyful text. I see your work on Norval as being along the same lines. You don't leave him with us as either a tragic or revelatory figure. He's deeply human. I see the possibilities for Indigenous work as being as open and variegated as each of our stories.

Ruffo: I agree wholeheartedly. Futurisms, healing, regeneration: that's where we have to go with our writing and, above all, our lives. As it stands, the more tragically we present ourselves the more the mainstream public laps it up when indeed we should be focusing on alternatives. *Granta* recently published a poem of mine called "The Reckoning" in their Canada issue, and although it may appear at first reading to be tragic, what I'm saying is that the health of the planet and the very survival of humankind is contingent on Western society realizing that in attempting to destroy Indigenous cultures, they have come a breath away from destroying themselves and the planet. Case in point: microplastics have now infected the whole ecosystem. Their society is simply unsustainable. I suppose many people realize this and that's why Western culture is generally so nihilistic. And, yes, Norval Morrisseau for all his trauma and addictions was a remarkable visionary who recognized this and set out to do something about it through his art. He always said that his paintings were icons meant to heal the world, and that's where the next generation, your generation, needs to go: less pain, more gain. As a science major you're probably familiar with the word "biophilia." It means a love of life and the living world—an affinity—though I prefer to think of it as kinship between humans and other life forms; it's that kind of mindset that will save this planet! Indigenous poets lead the way! I'll leave it at that. It's been great having this conversation with you. Chi-Miigwech.

Howard: It's been a true honour and pleasure, Armand. Chi-Miigwech.

THERE'S ALWAYS MORE FREEDOM
TO GO AFTER:

Sina Queyras and Canisia Lubrin

Canisia Lubrin: I'm thinking of inhibition in terms of the poet as practition-er. My consideration of this is particularly unsettled by my own late-coming to the "identity" of poet. I'm thinking of ways the totalizing* eros of "poet" could be different from the practice of poetry. Do you feel, or have you ever felt, in-hibited in that fabled sense? I wonder in particular what role inhibition plays in poetry: what it means to be a poet in the present moment.

(*I am willing to delay, and in some sense trouble, discernible contra-dictions that arise from shifting poet and poetry from absolute concentricity. In my thinking about this, I believe I always knew I was a poet even when I did not practise the form or its language.)

Sina Queyras: Inhibition is a humbling place to begin our conversation, Ca-nisia, and I love that I can find my name in yours, by the way. Your comment about "knowing" you were a poet even before "practising" the art is an inter-esting one and falls into one of the cracks in the foundation of poetry which, as I see it in any case, is the difference between a poetics of mastery (learned) and a poetics of inquiry (instinctive). Or, perhaps more specifically, a poetics of "concreteness" versus "groundlessness," which the Buddhists say is where kindness comes from.

I don't know that I've been caught up in the myth or fable of the poetic fig-ure myself, or how I conceive of the figure of the poet in all of its many guises. Do you mean the kinds of poet-figures we raise up with our attention? The ravisher, the rake, the tragic, the mystic, the naturalist, the elegist, the wise, the crone, the sculptor, the dancer? I mean, we have so many figureheads to try on, right?

On the other hand, I admit to being overly reverent of the idea of "poet." I take the title very seriously and see it as holding meaning far beyond having simply written the poem. I'm also a bit suspicious. I have always "feared" I was a poet. It has been something I have actively resisted. I went to school not to further entrench myself as poet, for example, but to learn to write beyond poetry. To feel free to express myself in any form or genre I chose. So you see, my own perception of myself as poet is quite fraught and has been about learning self-acceptance. What does Suzuki Roshi say? "Each of *you* is *perfect* the way *you* are ... and *you* can use a *little improvement.*"

Lubrin: How cool about our names.

It's to our great fortune, then, that the more these distinctions of what is raised up or dismissed or "high" or "low" become blurred, the greater the variety of poetry we have through which to view the world. This is, to my mind, an antidote to the disproportionate institutionalizing of poetry, which has pulled poetry quite a bit away from its true home: the people, the streets, the non-expert. I am more concerned here for agency as it pertains to a poetic practice than I am for the contradictions that mark the colonial haphazardness of my own life and upbringing. This chiaroscuro may be at the heart of this reticence that I am attempting to underscore, then. Something happens in the intersection where poetry and the poet exist that is both prismatic and invitational.

In true companionship the poem should find its reader. The poem is uneasy with the poet; the poet won't let it rest; the poet asks everything of the poem; we are endlessly demanding and we are irreconcilable with our creation. Perhaps this is as it should be. Conversely, the theorist is ever diagnostic, ever forensic and the poem is uneasy there, too. Give the poem its reader and the poem lives. What I'm getting at here is a way to think through the mobility of language in paradox. A simultaneous grounding and levity in the instinct, purpose and application of language in the form of poetry. This sentiment is expressed in your poem "Progress" from *Expressway*, though in the context of reckoning with the paradox of choice and/or choicelessness. The ideation of art, the gift and how it considers its dissemination in the consumerist mode. Of course, to examine how much control we give up in any creative mode, and how illusory our ideas of progress, is really to face the limits of all art.

Queyras: I like what you say about the poem coming for you. It's true. You can't always control what you write next. *Expressway* for example was never an easy project. It's America. 9/11. Ambition. Patriarchy. Capitalism. Romanticism. Racism. The failure of those belief systems. The terror of complicity and unconsciousness. Our bubbles. Living in America from 2000 to 2007, I had a sense, always, a very visceral sense of the number of bodies required for a given mile of road, a given product, a job, a house. It all seemed very measured. Very intentional. America is a place where the cost of the system is always obvious and also accepted. It's the same in Canada and I have had a lived sense of the cost of my own life in relation to those around me (perhaps because as a child we moved so often and I always felt like a guest in whatever community I inhabited). But in those post-9/11 moments it felt as though someone had torn my eyes open to an even more intense degree and I could not sleep. Moving to Philadelphia was, in a way, the final straw. The divisions there, the lines: racial, economic, the pockets of privilege so neatly cordoned off. Differently policed. I felt very, very conflicted. The poets on the ground, C.A. Conrad and Frank Sherlock, for example, experiencing such precariousness, literally no health care at that time, no safety net of any kind, and privilege—largely white—floating in on the train from New York. I could not live with the extreme contradictions.

So yes, it *is* a matter of connecting our ideas with our art, our values with our choices on the page and with our feet and heartbeats. What does being embodied cost? What does our practice cost? Our jobs? Our families? Our communities? My sister passed away a few months back. It's not lost on me that with each book I've published I have moved further and further from my roots. And with each I have suffered a literal death in my family, a tearing away and a severing of myself from my family of origin.

The cost is always on my mind. I think it's ironic that I came to poetry to express something of the experience of being in my body growing up in a precarious, working-class world—coming through the pain of my parents' loss of their first-born at fifteen, their tumultuous marriage, their inability to stabilize (you feel like you're under water for such a long time; you're just awash in other people's decisions, their economies and systems)—and that expression has cost me whatever tenuous connection remained. Possibly even my connection to myself. By that I mean: as a child I felt deeply but couldn't articulate what was happening in the body—not my child body, not the mother body, or the sibling body, or the friend body. I recall very clearly the day my oldest brother died: walking outside and staring up at the elm tree as if there was some significance in it. Something that could soothe or tell. That moment is one of my poetic bedrocks. That swell of time I entered into. Looking to "nature" for solace. That groundlessness. I was never able to be part of the dream after that. Not really. I always saw myself as disconnected from domestic life.

Lubrin: Let me offer condolences on the death of your sister and the many others throughout your life. Loss is one of those things that catalyzes my writing as well and it is something with which I am so intimately connected that I fear I know loss more than anything or anyone else. I lost my best friend, who was also my niece, when I was five and then, it seemed, in quick succession throughout the years, more and more people dear to me. Interestingly, this is also how I found writing. My grandmother (whom I also lost early in my life) ushered me into the world of language and music and story. That experience is at the bedrock of my writerly sensibilities. Later poetry would introduce me to many pluralities that I wouldn't have encountered otherwise, including the plurality of loss. Poetry offered many paths through living with loss. It took years for me to realize how my writing has benefited from this sense of loss: from my ensuing armouring of my life and from my eventual disarming. Loss often gets characterized as only trauma and I find this limiting. I've been thinking a lot lately about formulations in much of Western art that (re)circulate trauma as commodity through performative methods of ownership, disablement and dissemination. Those things underscore a particularly colonial attitude toward art that insists upon redemption narratives. I tend to want to transmute loss out of its own logic and from its own insistence away from that stuff: no, I do not have a Zion theorized for you and I do not offer any maps to get there. Do that work yourself.

Queyras: Thanks Canisia, and I am still processing the "best friend" who was also your "niece." My parents came from families of eight and ten children so this is not surprising to me. I was once in the same class as my cousin and her "aunt," who was my second cousin I suppose. I started out with five siblings. I have lost four. I have to say, it has been difficult and a bit numbing. There's an Oscar Wilde line, "losing one sibling is terrible, two is a tragedy, anything more than that starts to seem like carelessness…" I hear you on the walls: can't get hurt if you don't love, but man, it hurts to *not* love.

Lubrin: Yet that state of wakefulness might be the most important in poetry. It is tied to the intensity of perception required for good poetry to come about. The human cost and gain on every front are so real, both for those strictly toiling in the systems and the "isms" that create such dissociative civilizations and for those who make art within those structures. What is the price for poets, who we can assume are aware of the cost of making conscious choices, to write out of those simplifying structures the complexities that survive us and that we survive?

I remember the moment in which I first read Audre Lorde's essay "Poetry Is Not a Luxury." I remember what I was doing, what tea I was drinking, what I was wearing. This was a visceral opening up of something vast in my mind. You're likely familiar with it and how she posits her idea that poetry is in itself a way for women (especially those historically and contemporaneously marginalized) to survive because poetry offers a particular kind of freedom: emotional freedom. That the woman's voice and voicing(s) and the woman's feelings are radical and can be put to revolutionary use.

In Lorde's expressed relationship with poetry, I met my own preoccupations with poetry's activist invigorations and ceaseless reach. I knew much of the same stuff instinctively and could practise its modes within the contours of my own sense of poetic time and urgency. But when I approach a poem, I expect turbulence; I expect the turbulence of reaching for a freedom that is in itself undefined, to, in a sense, disrupt the process of writing. So here I am in some kind of practice that is interminable because the work of liberation is never done. There's always more freedom to go after and for me this is a searing kind of joy and trust in language in which everything is bound up. That there will always be poems to write is a thing that brings me immense purpose.

Queyras: That essay was published when I was in my early twenties. All the women I knew were busy doing social or political work. We worked in shelters with street kids, with women in the courts, defending women in divorce, helping to start community credit unions and co-op housing. I have this image of a long line of women drinking tea but with their fists in the air. Helen Portrebenko was the local poet everybody read then, and Adrienne Rich of course. It was freedom, yes, but also a *lot* of work. Everyone had a poetry broadside on a wall in their kitchen. Poetry was not about prize culture. Poetry was certainly not a luxury; it was about *surviving*.

I like what you say about each poem finding its reader. I was moved by the poetry I was surrounded by at the time, but I didn't feel *joy*, or even a glimmer of my own voice until I discovered Virginia Woolf, and that was very, very difficult because of the class, the privilege: reading Woolf was like reading a foreign language. The narrative seemed to be taking place above my head. But hers was a language that unlocked an entire ecosystem in myself that I had never been able to access. I lay on the floor in my small house on Vancouver Island, absolutely, beautifully perplexed by *The Waves*. It was my before-and-after book and I went on to read everything over and over again. My love of Woolf was mysterious for many, many years and it fed me. It was a tremendous motivator just scrambling after her, and then realizing I was actually scrambling after myself.

Lubrin: That image you invoke of a long line of women drinking tea with their fists in the air characterizes, for me, what underwrites your opus. I am imbued with that sense of defiance and carrying-on-living in your lines and that makes for some radical awakening in language. My moment of rapture came with reading Dionne Brand's *No Language Is Neutral*. My ecosystem, if I can borrow your phrase, was completely lost in a darkness I could not ever be compassed out of until that moment. I realized my own oddities, my own queer and troubled cohabitation with language as I had been conditioned in.

So in *Voodoo Hypothesis* I arrived at an awareness that I was staring into something inimical and attempting to dismantle it. The poems in the book exist in nonlinear time like pinballs, searching for brief illuminations to their questions before quickly moving on to unknown dispersals of their/my family tree before they must, inevitably, end. But there is nothing to hold the poems and lines too long in place. No guarantor to afford them a cleanly locatable thesis about what they mean to be. To have faith or to belong, to be free, to really live, is the greatest hope. An irony is the greater teacher, though. This suggestion of unbelonging can in some ways scaffold one's sense of truer positioning.

The stuff that determines a belief in belonging extends to speech. And since language is inherent to the project of poetry, whose every ache and luminosity is music, the song and celebration premised in the mode of its creation is troubled by a faith in words. Offered here are the polyvocal rhythms of tracing the creolized landscapes that riddle the West through the immense gravity of our colonial history. Offered, too, is a geography peopled through the very act of mining the complexly unique, simultaneously exilic and concentric circumstances of diaspora. People charged by their own insistence to be alive and to be. But with a place to disembark, yet without a place to claim and to be tethered to, *here* is, eventually, to reckon a re-entering into humanity, into speech, into body, into life beyond the trauma of unbelonging and even death. The Black body, then, is undeniably always the modern self. This is the project of *Voodoo Hypothesis* and it is one that resists any sure categorization because to be alive in the Black diaspora is to be in constant, "conscious" flux.

Queyras: Yes, yes, yes to Dionne Brand, and yes to that experience of discovering *No Language Is Neutral*. A very important book. And it's fascinating to me the way you describe bodies pinging off of colonial structures—I get that sense in your work completely and quite distinctly. The endless surf/state/corporation pounding. It is the way *capitalism*, which so often seems just a stand-in for *whiteness*, appears to subsume everything and break whatever commodity it accumulates into ever smaller portions to sell back to itself. Poetry can be a way to stop and turn and confront that force. A way to resist. Or, as Anne Boyer said a while back, "Capitalism couldn't work if souls did…"

In a sense, for me, these moments mine that early plunge into a non-linear world. The mind-meld of a poem offers oxygen. A way to "wake up" as the Buddhists say. And the counter-intuitive logic of letting go is so important. Of doing nothing. To not reach out, but to remain stable but fluid (I'm thinking of Sloterdijk's idea of the foam). To breathe. To feel. To face. Facing the moment is freedom. I love that line in Lorde's essay about "the white fathers" who "told us, I think therefore I am; and the black mothers in each of us—the poet—whispers in our dreams," asserting "I feel therefore I can be free." Not to decouple thinking and feeling, but to understand their essential relationship, which is, I think, poetry, or to my mind, the *potential* of poetry. The potential to be beautiful but resist ornamentation.

Obviously this is distinct from activism. Distinct from putting one's body on the line. Speaking metaphorically, this is the body, but also the poem. All of this relates equally to both. The line we walk in our day, the lines we write in our poems. Like you, Dionne Brand's *No Language Is Neutral* blew my pores open. Her vital moral presence vibrates in every lush syllable. And this question of dancing between joy and activism is found there and in Juliana Spahr's *Fuck You-Aloha-I Love You* or Claudia Rankine's *Don't Let Me Be Lonely: An*

American Lyric or Lisa Robertson's *The Weather*, which I felt like an apprentice to for a few years and now cannot read without feeling in conversation with Dionne Brand. Each of those writers has a natural rhythm that is incantatory and powerful in the way it accumulates and brings in and holds everything both outside and inside—the interiority is vast and vertical, but the sweep is so wide and generous—that sums up my goal as a writer nicely. No fear. Open to everything.

I immediately sensed something similarly deep and wide and direct with *Voodoo Hypothesis*, a book that offers such a tremendous canvas and wide caverns of thinking that have clearly been processed over time. I hear those various rhythms echoed in your work, traces of the many tongues that have tied the islands over our long colonial history. And the way bodies appear in these poems, we can trace them tunneling through, on the march, trying to re-enter their own "humanity," their own "bodies," their own "tongues." That call to give the bodies back. It's big. It's a very big first book and it lingers on the physical and material in ways that I think evidence a risk in the way our poetry can be activist. I think of Dionne Brand's *Ossuaries*, for example, which is—well, what can anyone say? I remain suspicious of poetry, lyric poetry, that is not capable of wide openness unless that inwardness is also doing something radical in its negotiations. Was this something you wrestled with? The "I"? And is this related to your statement about the Black body being the modern body? A rejection of whiteness? Of the way in which whiteness erases other bodies?

Lubrin: This characterization of *Voodoo Hypothesis* you present, I think, is well negotiated such that I may not need to add much more. The book's project is a vast undertaking that calls for a number of things to come into being. I believe it is a back turned to whiteness rather than a rejection of whiteness because to reject whiteness is also to inadvertently centre it through opposition. There's a lot of work out there rejecting whiteness. But the Black body in diaspora is the modern body because it exists in modernity before time. It is already beyond circumstance. It ushers in the next thing—the future, if you will—through sheer creative force even when it is given none of the credit. Whiteness is a construction that needs to be thrown in the fire and I am not speaking back to its conservatism. It is mainly concerned with status quo; its logic is colonial and capitalist, and quite frankly, bullshit. Traversing the troubled spaces of history, pain—in particular, Black pain—of the ethico-political conditions of belonging and belief, my book attempts to elucidate the complex work of creating in, living in and negotiating the work of diaspora. In particular, I sit with this myth of the Black Other (forged in imperialist logic) in a room spanning epochs, disciplines, literatures, cultures and attempt to throw some thinking, some light, some music about its vast and unimaginable costs. In this, I don't intend to assuage readers with pristine, untroubled clarity. My work situates a particular creolization which presents a far more interesting and important project. It wrestles with the ecstasy, possibility and cost of existing in a world in which anyone's humanity could be hypothetical. So, I don't intend to assuage the status quo. This is possibly why I did not publish any of my early work—those works were behaving according to what had already been established and because of the environment that I was writing in their creolité was always critiqued as opacity or characterized as "strangeness." This says a lot about who can access what in a work.

Voodoo Hypothesis undertakes that *what if* in the chaos and candour and prismatic challenges of Black life in this diaspora whose systems of personal and social value create realities for Black people anathema to these very proclamations. Diaspora is a place profoundly creative and great in its own right. I encounter this again and again in Dionne Brand's work and how it is in conversation, and creolizes, with other works variously located in the Black diaspora. In as much as *Voodoo Hypothesis* is a kind of poetic inquiry, I did not want to remove the contradictions inherent to its condition, nor did I mean to provide answers. I meant the poems to astound as the conditions that created them do in life. A reaching for clarity that is (yet) findable is part of the work of language and that is the challenge of the book to readers. I very much trust the reader to navigate those challenges, not in me, but in themselves. I do not write toward congratulatory comprehension; I'm writing freedom and there is hardly a more illogical, necessary, more difficult and rewarding undertaking. In a world that has had all of its so-called progresses built on the mere illusion of freedom and virtue, it is all of our responsibility to wade toward the truer logic of a world for *all of us*. So, you are right. I have had decades to think about this stuff.

In terms of the lyric "I": I have always wrestled with it. I still wrestle with it. I find the "I" unknowable but also too eager, too sure. But that's my mess to sort out. I still trust in the work that the "I" presents. Poetry tends toward beauty, and beauty might be anatomically inextricable from art. Why else do we go to art if not in search of beauty? And why must beauty be characterized hegemonically? Why not see the world as both beauty and dread in their infinite variations, entanglements and interactions? Where does beauty take us?

Queyras: Oh yes, the "unknowable" "too eager" "I"—it always seems to be centring itself in the poem. Making pretty. Making nice. It's the earnestness, the speaker as the "awake" one, the one above the implications of the seeing "I" that I find troubling in lyric poetry. I love a moral, essential core in a poem/poet, but don't want to encounter righteousness, which is for me the less pleasing aspect of call-out culture. The tone of anger is difficult to negotiate, of course. "Come in to the poem," she says, jaws wide (and grinning). But the poetry I love always turns its back on those easy formulas in favour of complexity.

Bullshit indeed. I am amazed by the degree to which we have been indoctrinated by these notions of whiteness. I feel your description above, of the possibility of new lives and formulations in the chaos or the open space of the poems you are writing. My aims are similar, describe or create the space you want to inhabit, but I mourn somehow the work of the poems (essential as it is). There has not been enough pleasure. Wherever I go next must be filled with joy. Joyful poetry has seemed to me the real luxury and something I have railed against because so often it appears totally delusional. I'm thinking of a tussle I got into with Lisa Robertson and others during a post-reading Q & A in Calgary at which she claimed (after I said I felt compelled to end *Expressway* on a note of hope) that hope was immoral.

Hope is like joy. I am always in awe, envious of poets who can rest in joy or arrive at joy because it's easy to write off joy as delusion. Not facing up to the real. But a poet who can rest in the "I" and in the full depth of pain using the wealth of poetry and not simply reeling under the pummel of it—as you describe in relation to your project. That's what I am looking for (and, ironically, Lisa Robertson is one such poet). Not avoiding, but moving into and through, creating new pathways, new spaces. Maybe hope is a kind of avoidance? In any case, how do we move forward carrying the weight of our dead? How do we move forward not carrying the weight of our dead? This is what I have been negotiating throughout my work.

I recognize something of your powerful repudiation of whiteness, too, though I am, of course, white. But even inside this skin whiteness appears an apparition. Also blinding. So how to sing myself? Not so easy. Still, poetry is song. And love. And beauty. And despite everything (end times in every direction) I love life and feel the need to bite through. I constantly need to remind myself that I can have joy. That I can have beauty, both in verse and in life. I did not feel I had the right to access joy in verse as a contemporary queer, othered, outside body until I read Marilyn Hacker's *Love, Death, and the Changing of the Seasons.* Then I realized that lyric song and poetic tools were not necessarily the enemy. That there could be pleasure and eros and pain all in the same line—and it could be activist, or activated in terms of interrogating the status quo, but also awash, even dripping with beauty. There's a way in which your wry but constant perspective does this too. And hearing you read I found a similar hum or weave to the way Brand or Robertson inhabit a reading, which is to say, a "brocade" of sound. How aware of the reading process are you in writing?

Lubrin: Whiteness is not white skin, whiteness is imagined. We are all under siege by it. And the fact that is has created such havoc is a hard lesson in the power of the imagination when it is usurped into toxic, world-spanning structures and ideas.

On to reading as process: I am extremely aware of it but that awareness isn't capitulated, it is made from the stuff of the music, the songs of poetry, so perhaps it is one and the same as writing. But I don't read poetry when I write poetry because the result is a kind of sensory overload. I do read many different kinds of texts throughout the drafting process: books from nearly any genre other than poetry. I need to be able to feel freely and too much of the same kind of energy tends to limit how poetry happens for me. I need to hear my own lines, syllables, voice and mood so I can angle these into creating the poem and committing to its frequency, its felt senses. There are, however, poets whose musicality awaken some sensibility in me: Dionne Brand, Lucille Clifton, Gwendolyn Brooks, Aimé Cesairé, Derek Walcott, Adrienne Rich, Audre Lorde, Kamau Brathwaite, Kwame Dawes, Wole Soyinka and many Spanish poets, Reina María Rodríguez for instance—her *Time's Arrow* is an exquisite work. Your own work, Sina. Several peers: Aisha Sasha John, Phoebe Wang, Vladimir Lucien, Safiya Sinclair, Danez Smith, Solmaz Sharif, Juliane Okot Bitek, Bardia Sinaee, Ishion Hutchinson and others. These poets are all holding dynamic spaces within their own rattled courtships with language and feeling and thought in poetry.

I will say I don't quite know if a resolution exists or is needed for the lyric "I" and its tendency to beautify, per se. Beauty in our world is needed, can be revolutionary and remains a catalyst for good. I think the accusation is that when an assumed void or a thing that lacks "inherent" beauty is filled with the beautiful, it can be unsettling, especially in language. The poet is accused of pretense or indulgence but I tend to want to avoid thinking about disunity as a flaw. What else is possible? What new thing am I constantly reaching for? An accusation, yet again, is leveled at the poet's sensibility. Is it not true that meaning is *made* between the poem and the reader, not simply or exclusively because craft dictates a certain engagement/interpretation?

Queyras: Well, hear hear to disunity "not" being a flaw and to not buying into the commodity of whiteness and to continuing to query who and what is celebrated and to challenging the notion of poetic *expression* above creating a specific kind of poetry. Despite the current dumpster fire of "CanLit," we are in a golden moment for poetry and I sense that we're only at the beginning. I sense too, the emergence of a generation of skilled critical writers from a wide variety of aesthetic backgrounds and with very distinct political goals. I have seen so many incredible debut collections in the past few years including yours, Phoebe Wang's, Billy-Ray Belcourt's, Joshua Whitehead's, Stevie Howell's, Jordan Abel's and I'm looking forward to Tess Liem's, which I know to be spectacular. Not to mention our American friends, some of whom you mention, and also Ocean Vuong, Tommy Pico and so many others. And those essayists: Alicia Elliott, Haley Mlotek, Durga Chew-Bose. There's a *lot* to be angry about, but there's also a *lot* to be excited about. When I started *Lemon Hound* we were in a very different world. Now I'm not sure it's needed anymore.

Congrats on your long-listings for all three League of Canadian Poets awards, by the way. That brings an entirely different sort of light on the work. I feel like we also live in a time when it's almost impossible not to be caught up in the small spotlight of poetry: the prize lists and the reviews. The only time non-poets speak to me of poetry is about prizes. It's difficult to maintain a sustaining practice in that spotlight, I think. How are you holding up?

Lubrin: Thank you, Sina. I do not read reviews of my work. I made one exception for a new reviews website founded by two peers out of Montreal because I'm interested in their motivations. Their sense of reviewing resists the dominant, clinical, aesthetic-war-driven tradition that seems to characterize criticism in Canadian Letters. I think, too, that my reaction to the awards nominations is still pending. I do not write with awards juries in mind but since the book is getting that kind of attention, I have to admit I am happy for the book. Some things live even in spaces that can't yet recognize them.

You're right about simplistic responses to problems. The goal should be equality, not a thing that behaves equitably while carrying on with the same old destructive structures. The same old logics at work, the same old constitutions at play, and for what? What outcome other than reshuffling the same old mess? The current upheaval is evidence that things are shifting in important ways.

I think I have written a book that complicates our present iteration of prize logic/culture. I know that the book's effect is clear, but its multimodal enactment of form is puzzling. People might sense that there is something in the work that warrants reward (based on whatever prize logic) but what I've done is booby-trap the book for anyone looking to easily consume "blackness." So it's not an easy book.

I think there could be better models for recognition other than the currently normalized version of prize culture. My focus, then, is squarely on the work and in what life is next for me in language. I am always writing, even when I'm not sure what I'm writing. Is this sense of unknowing present for you, say in the writing of your most recent work *My Ariel*, or do you need to be aware of the work's purpose from the get-go?

Queyras: Yes, you are smart to avoid reviews, and avoid "CanLit." Reviews and categories such as "CanLit" are generally about something other than either one's work or the world one comes out of and writes into, and I am happy to see them challenged. To remain on the page. That's the difficulty. I have pinned photos of Agnes Martin with her back to the world and Yayoi Kusama with brush in hand and Louise Bourgeois with one of her soft sculptures—these are artists I respect tremendously. Artists whose practice has a rich consistency that is visceral and playful yet consistent and demanding and long-term. I have to imagine that the millions of humans around the world, whether winding thread or kneading dough or cleaning a window or making soup, find pleasure in the joy of repeated actions done with full concentration. That's the only way what we, as poets, do makes sense to me. I mean, there has to be the moment of communion at the end, whether it's breaking bread or letting the light in.

But to the purpose of poetry: I found that in *My Ariel* the purpose continually morphed as conditions in my immediate world heated up and my own expectations were met; just as I had achieved one goal, it seemed to vanish, to appear not only unrealized but in some cases absent. The poems, or at least some of them, came to seem like engagement without end. I could still be rewriting "Morning Song." I could rewrite "Morning Song" every day of my life and perhaps not feel I had achieved *the* version, one that matched the completeness of Plath's. This was disconcerting.

MORNING SONG
Sina Queyras

A love procedure set me going like a big fat lie.
An IT specialist slapped a motherboard
And my first bald Tweet slid into the feed.

All night Instagrams and updates Flickr
In pixellated dreams. I wake to a beep, stumble
Out in my men's nightshirt and stare, blank as a gull,

Into the liquid crystal display.
Am I any more authentic than the account
That Tweets your verse?

Or the cloud that archives your words?
Or the screen on which your poems float?
Dickinson says to fill a gap, insert the thing that caused it.

What thing? This sleek app that brightens
And swallows my thoughts? These two moons
That fill my palms and eat my hours?

Vowels rise and hover like drones.
What is missing in me? Refresh. Refresh.
I can't stop searching for love here.

Having said that, I never know where I am going. I know what I want to explore in a project, I know the constraint or the material, but I am discovering just as the reader is discovering. What makes a text "complete" and "buoyant"? This is what I find perplexing about the relationship between form and content. There have been projects where I have felt satisfied with the outcome— *Lemon Hound* and *MxT*, for example, *Expressway* to some degree. And why? I think this sense of satisfaction has something to do with reception and effect, which after all is usually aligned with what an artist has compressed into the writing process. But for me, the writing of the book never leaves my body. What my body went through.

When I read "Lacking the Wind's Higher Reasoning" and "Polite Uncertainty," I am faced with the feeling of bodies trapped in corridors. Bodies between power sources. Bodies confronting power. The marvel of posture despite the verticality of power. I mean, there's a certain laissez-faire that I associate with a privileged position in poetry. The wealth of a poetics can seem loud and lush, but not about "wealth" in a way that my in-laws might recognize. The wealth of poetic engagement that is lost when the poem leaves the body. I like this notion of a "multi-modal enactment" of form that you were puzzling with in *Voodoo Hypothesis*. Did you achieve your goal?

POLITE UNCERTAINTY
Canisia Lubrin

for Bianca Spence

Let me see you
leave with your
posture of stones.
Or pray, if you must, to your lit
from both ends artillery
where the world is reduced
to the height of your nose.
Best yet: is grazed on the boundary of your toes.
Your local memory, your pause, cannot suddenly sag my syllables,

or whatever you trip upon outside
myself being invaded–but no–
who reduced you to the work
of a tilted head, and respite, pardon my flare, stretching the lips, polite?

But uncertain as what borrows now, as always, the dread mock of beauty
fusing mindlessly, the Morse code to the hieroglyph, the telegraph to the
Braille, the dying serif to the pixelated phrase,
throw the uproar the swallowed whole, the history as font.

Tell me how to be funny. Tell me how I haven't tried.
Lend me your gaze.
Let me sign, stupidly, your name:

Lubrin: Very interesting points regarding repeated action and the result of this repetition in the body. Each poem is a different way of leaning into the world so it never feels like a repeated action to me; writing a poem is always a new encounter with language, writing and form. The grounding work of craft that must be returned to again and again is a kind of posture perhaps, but exhaustion after writing is always a part of the process for me. I then need to recalibrate, clear my mind and reposition myself in the world, in my body.

Both "Polite Uncertainty" and "Lacking the Wind's Higher Reasoning" attempt to engage in a kind of reclaiming of the self. I tend to want to go after the always multivalent when I write; even when the only thing I want to do is burn my poems, the fire I face isn't always the same. *Voodoo Hypothesis* is an uneasy work. I think this is its mode, its puzzle, its form. The book came about through line-by-painstaking-line of putting conscious pressure on language at the edge of the unconscious—the work then becomes apparent. Writing is living for me, so this book isn't fettered to a goal, it is simply aware of itself.

Queyras: Consciousness. That's where it's at.

THE VOICE ASKING:

Dionne Brand and
Souvankham Thammavongsa

Souvankham Thammavongsa: Dionne, we've known each other for some time.

Dionne Brand: A long time in the practice of poetry.

Thammavongsa: Can you tell me a memory you have of me?

Brand: It's a memory of first noticing your handwriting and exclaiming at the precision, geometry and economy of it and you telling me a story of a childhood where you learned to write under a light in precise economical cursive. I like your minimalism, which is why I wanted to have this conversation with you.

Thammavongsa: Handwriting can be so revealing. It gives so much away. You see me.

Brand: It was meticulous and spare yet it filled the page; it made use of every corner. It was a notebook.

Thammavongsa: Notebooks are so expensive. I wanted what I wrote to fill up any space I could find. Clean paper to write on is a currency. I didn't have much of it.
   You just had a birthday. Was it a good one?

Brand: I don't like or dislike birthdays. There are many events, public or publicly private, that one is supposed to celebrate and enjoy—there is an expectation that one shares the same feeling, and the "right" feeling, around these events. They can be public holidays or events like birthdays. I've never been able to understand their significance outside of what seems a moral imposition. I don't care if people remember my birthday and that is why I have to write people's birthdays down in case I offend them by not remembering, because I am so neutral on birthdays myself. But of course I have birthday parties and such just to appear normal. Just as I vote in solidarity with my friends who believe in democracy but otherwise am totally cynical, if not yet indifferent, to politicians. Plus I like poetry and I like to dance so this is what I usually ask people to do at a birthday party.

Thammavongsa: I like going to a birthday party. It tells me a lot about the person who is having the party: who they consider their friends, who they love, what their family is like, what gifts they are happy to receive, who isn't invited, who they ask to dance. Who am I to be here? I like to sit next to a family member and hear stories the birthday-person would never tell about themselves.

What age do or did you enjoy being?

Brand: I don't think I enjoy/enjoyed any age. All ages are full of anxiety. I enjoy periods of any year. Sometimes a whole year is horrendous but "thank heavens for the earth and the sky" as it says in one of my poems, "all indifferent all unconcerned."

Thammavongsa: You also say the author is in place and not in time. Time is simultaneous and forever unfolding, changing. Age is about place.

Brand: And the reverse. The author lives in time and not in place. Place is gravity, it holds the body and as you say time is more volatile. It doesn't observe the same rules as place.

Thammavongsa: Who are you excited to read?

Brand: Anyone from South America, anyone from anywhere in the world other than where I am. Located in North America leaning right upon the behemoth of the USA, it is difficult not to see that living and those concerns as central, or at least all of the publishing industry operates as if the generally white and middle-class subject is the subject of literature—that extends to Britain too—that the English-speaking subject is the subject to address, and that subject and its concerns are invariably white and male. John Keene, his *Counternarratives* is superb; Nikki Wallschlaeger, shockingly clear and bright lines; Ludmilla Petrushevskaya, she is so funny and pitiless; Horacio Castellanos Moya; Yuri Herrera; NoViolet Bulawayo; Fiston Mwanza Mujilla's *Tram 83* is a post-technological waste, post-resource extraction novel—it is not dystopian, it is post-post-dystopian. Amazing. In reading I really want to know what is going on in the world in other lives discerned with other sensibilities—I'm not interested in anything I know already.

Thammavongsa: Readers, when they read only what they know, have such a narrow view of humanity, of hope, of each other. That's not what reading is supposed to do.

Brand: And you, who are you excited to read and why?

Thammavongsa: I love NoViolet Bulawayo too! The way she describes snow, and how she writes a child's voice. That anger, I recognize myself in it. Laila Slimani; I loved *The Perfect Nanny*. She gives everything away in the first two sentences of the novel and she's so good that you don't even care. It's supposed to be a thriller—well, sort of—but it's a wonderful observation on race and class. Ottessa Moshfegh is so great. I love everything she's written. I love how she writes about the body and how grotesque it is. Her characters have pimples and are so ugly, but they are the heroes of the story. Why can't a hero be so grotesque and so utterly human, too? Krysada Binly Panusith Phounsiri, Madhur Anand—they have other things outside of the poetry. Binly has a degree in physics and travels the world as a breakdancer. David Sedaris because he is so funny and how he can handle something so utterly heartbreaking. He writes wonderful invectives. It's very hard to do. I like Rupi Kaur for what she means to poetry. Everything I had ever been told about it, she proves it's not true, you don't have to be that or go that way. She means something to me because once when I had mentioned I was a Canadian poet, I was told, "That's nothing." I was so humiliated for having thought myself one and then humiliated because I didn't say anything back because of the possibility that maybe it was a valid point about me. Whatever she is, she is not nothing. And no one can say that to her. I love that about her. I recently read Terese Marie Mailhot's memoir, *Heart Berries*. I love how small it is. You can write a life and it can be a small book, but it can feel so big, such immense and startling power. Sarah Kabamba, Doretta Lau, Brit Bennett. Jenny Zhang. Ada Limón, Natalie Diaz, Mai Der Vang, Emma Cline, Tennessee Williams.

But I know most of these writers are North American and I know my reading is limited; after all, there is so much a book and words can do. I really like what's happening in film and television and art. Kulap Vilaysack, she writes for television and also recently made a documentary film called *Origin Story*. She's so funny and again can handle sadness within that funny. Ali Wong. I love her show on Netflix. She's also writing a memoir—a series of letters to her daughter. I can't wait to read that. Alex Cu Unjieng is so wonderful. I adore her drawings and prints and her aesthetic. She was handing out stickers of vaginas she drew. I love how serious and real and funny and also so very poignant her work is.

I also like to "read" real living people—what I mean by that is people who are just walking by, having a fight in a restaurant, or my family, or the people sitting across from me when they come in to have me prepare a tax return. But I should end it here on what I'm excited to read. It's getting too long.

Brand: I'm laughing hearing you say it's getting too long—for a minimalist. But I know what you mean about living people. I was walking through a parking lot and a man dressed in winter clothing on a very hot day, obviously distressed, was repeating to himself a line from the Christian Bible that became a Bob Marley lyric, which it seemed was also a complaint about how he had been treated: "Who God bless let no man curse." Then as I walked on I heard a man telling a woman, "When Jack calls what does he usually want? When Jack calls what does he usually want?" And so on that morning—momentous things were being said.

Thammavongsa: Meaning. Do you begin with it, hold it in mind, or does it arrive later, independent of you?

Brand: Everything begins in meaning, which is different from conclusion. I think even if we haven't discerned it or chosen it or known it we begin in meaning—that is we begin in the world. So it may arrive independent of me, so to speak, because I have no control of all of it, only what floods into me and what I then manage to see through the lens of my experience, the knowledges I've gathered.

Thammavongsa: Meaning doesn't conclude. That is why it means and continues to mean. I wrote something down once, just to record it, that did not make sense to me at the time but many years later reading it over I understood what was said to me. And there was no way to go back to that meaning.

What surprises you?

Brand: Racism. Every time. No matter my experiences, no matter all the data. It shocks me. I am a perpetual innocent against it. I just can't believe it. I am always speechless before it. This innocence opens one for brutality. At the same time, if I were as grim as racists and racism, the world would be totally lost because I would be as brutal too.

Thammavongsa: I'm brutal. I'm not surprised. That is racism, to be unsurprised, to expect it even. I'm surprised when someone is not racist. I'm speechless.

A perpetual innocent is really about love. Love for self, for others. To have no one take that from you, even in the face of brutality, is revolutionary.

Brand: I would like to get over this though. I can't bear being shocked all the time. It's like a blow to the face.

Thammavongsa: If you could have a single sentence to say over and over what would it be?

Brand: "Déjeme decirle, a riesgo de parecer ridículo, que el revolucionario verdadero está guiado por grandes sentimientos de amor." Che Guevara. In any language. "Let me say at the risk of seeming ridiculous, that the true revolutionary is guided by deep feelings of love."

Thammavongsa: Yes.

When you write, when does what you write become poetry or fiction? Are they different things to you?

They are not different to me. The people who are reading what I wrote are different. Sometimes what I write is fiction, but I am really writing poetry. It is always poetry.

Brand: Though I know what you mean, they are different processes to me. For me working in poetry is working exclusively in the material of language using sound, tension and accretion, compression and silence to gather meaning. The constraints of fiction may or may not be these, but poetry's constraints are always these. Of course, like you, I am always a poet writing a fiction so I am never without these particular constraints.

Thammavongsa: Describe an image of a place you've travelled, and why it's important to you to have been there.

Brand: The Atacama Desert. It was the quiet of it as soon as I arrived. This quiet settled everything I had been experiencing before; it quelled several years of disturbance.

Thammavongsa: Deserts are examples of maximalism. The quiet can be so large, so weighted, it is louder than any disturbance. I say this because it's how I like to think of my writing. The quiet, the silence, the nothing there is maximized. I make things bare and I amplify that.

Brand: It's wonderful that you say deserts are examples of maximalism. I had strangely thought minimalism! I wanted to go someplace empty of noise. You are right, the silence crowded out the disturbance.

You've been to a desert; what was it like for you?

Thammavongsa: Yes. In Marfa, Texas. The land was so flat. All I noticed was sky. It made me feel seasick. It was too much. And I loved the tumbleweeds. I was so happy to see them. I know that tumbleweeds began somewhere and they take the shape they have because nothing stood in the way of their tumbling-toward.

Brand: I went and I knew I would be at peace immediately or that something definitive would happen, and it did. Coming down from the El Tatio geysers there were mirages. Light and the lithium in the soil made the colour of the earth various. You could be anywhere. I saw the mirage of a harbour and my friend saw a forest.

Thammavongsa: It's so hard to know where you are in a desert. In a city, you can memorize a corner store, a building, a face, a lamppost, or all of these things together. In a desert, everything looks the same. Even something that marks you like your footprint, the wind takes care of that.

Brand: What city do you love?

Thammavongsa: New York. I just love walking for miles and miles. It makes sense to me that First Avenue is next to Second Avenue and Second Avenue is next to Third. I love Toronto too. But that is like saying I love my mother. It's not right not to. And maybe that annoys me a little. That I feel I have to say it.

Brand: I loved Cairo right away. And Delhi. Both for the same reason. People—so numerous, multitudinous in the streets. I loved being among so many bodies, zigzagging, crossing streets, breathing in a common way. An incredible feeling of mass and weight and commonality.

Thammavongsa: What are you doing when you are not writing? Like, do you watch television?

Brand: Reading. I haven't watched television for a long time. First I banished the TV to the basement and then I stopped watching it. I have to stop paying for cable since I don't use it. I only use it to watch tennis and World Cup soccer and the Tour de France and the Olympics—I'm a sports junkie, which is why I still have the TV, I suppose.

Thammavongsa: Dionne, I did not know this about you. I am a sports junkie as well. What I love about sports is how all answer *why* with *I must*. It doesn't make sense. Why cycle that far to get there, why hit the ball or run to that base, why twist your body four times in the air, why get in the ring? It's a lot like poetry. Why write this sentence or choose that word and put it there. *Because I must.*

What are you still learning about yourself as a writer?

Brand: Words I heard as a child suddenly have their true significance. The way my grandmother pronounced "lentil" in French patois, then the word "mamaguy" which was from the Spanish "mamagallista," meaning a teaser, joker or flatterer in our case. No remarks were ever made in my house about their origins—they were spoken seamlessly with English. They were in the language of the house. So I am learning now in another meaning. Childhood remains a mystery. Has it happened to you that you suddenly understand a word decades later?

Thammavongsa: Yes. We would get a lot of words wrong from English but we did not know they were wrong among ourselves. It is just how we said them, together, as a family. The way we got them wrong had a deepening to the language that, for me, would not have been there had we gotten them right. One word is *knife*. I was taught to pronounce the first letter because it is the first, it is there. I understand why, the reasoning behind it. My experience of that word means so much to me. It's just a letter, but what we got wrong about it is a story about how we lived. I'm also learning that I can't do things.

Brand: What things?

Thammavongsa: I can't show a reader in a visible way that what they are reading comes from a lot of work they can't see because there is so little on the page. That's the thing about minimalism. I can't show. I can only show this in feeling which is something we can't see.

I want the writing to feel like standing on the other side of a dam, the part where you don't feel the water but it is there, behind the wall, humming. It's the architecture and structural engineering that is keeping that water back. The end result looks minimal, but I had to create the water, had to put it there, build the dam—all of it—in order for that standing there to have meaning. When I'm writing about the small, something I found, or light, I am also writing about the other; that is to say, the big, what I lost, the dark…but it is the reader who must bring these in with them to enter the work.

A maximalist can see all of this. Though we call what we do different things, we see each other. Is this your experience?

Brand: Well, what we are calling maximalism here is for me compression of meaning and concentration of sound. I try to apply maximum pressure to the page by clasping words together in an unusual architecture or with an unusual speed, or by producing unusual sound. It requires, as with minimalism, attention to clarity. I am trying to be as clear as possible as each examined word is added. Every single word in the line matters and has a precise function—none can be merely administrative or casual or excessive.

Thammavongsa: I think what I mean to say is that minimalism or maximalism is something that happens somewhere else. For the writer, the thinking and the writing require the same sets of decisions.

As a reader, what are you still learning about yourself?

Brand: I notice now how I read. The pleasures are different. Now I read for structure, so the shape of the work is what gives me pleasure. Or the insight it accumulates. I am interested in the architecture of the work: what it borrows from, what it leaves unchanged from the past, how it breaks embedded narrative or not, how lazy or agile the poet. A dear friend poet asked me, a long time ago, "D, does the world need that line?" And it took me aback and then made me laugh and then made me measure each line of poetry I wrote against this question. Such a simple question and such a difficult one—bracing and settling.

Thammavongsa: And unsettling.

I'm learning that I haven't read enough. And what I love or pay attention to sometimes is not important to anyone but me. I'm not generous with what I read. I can love what I read but I realize I can be an angry reader. Sometimes I don't understand why someone published something, why it exists in the world. I want to be more generous that it has managed to exist. I understand that I'm not. And I know I can't pretend.

We always take note of a beautiful poem. I think we learn to be better writers when we understand what makes a bad one. What's a thing about a bad poem you learned from?

Brand: Fundamentally I respect every poem attempted. It is a sign of such faith in what cannot be lived, understood or communicated. So even bad poems, or weak poems, I appreciate. I don't like a pretentious poem though, a poem that announces a link to European traditions expecting a casual reference or clumsy and obsequious invocation of Keats or Shelley or ancient Greece to do the work of actual poetry making. A good poem collects or tries to collect all the difficulty of living, all the tension of being in that moment into one sound or one image and elicits a feeling that the poet and the reader have not had before. Or more radically, that the world has not had before. What's a beautiful poem for you and what's a bad poem?

Thammavongsa: All poems are bad, or at least they begin that way. But something happens to one and it isn't anymore. I don't know what that is, that thing that changes it. I recognize it when it's beautiful. And I don't know why it's beautiful. It's not something I can explain.

What's more important, talent or hard work?

Brand: Hard work, meaning hard reading. What do you think?

Thammavongsa: Hard work. I think anyone can have talent. When I was starting out, I was around many talented poets, poets more talented than me but I am still here.

This question became really important to me this year because I taught creative writing for the first time. I thought I knew. I had many talented students and there was one who was hopeless. But they showed up every single day and did not flinch when I told them the hard work they needed to do. The hopeless student had a longer way to come than all the others because this student had no talent. But this student put in hard work and understood they may never get to the level that those talented students were at, but they put in the work anyway. When the year was over, two of the most talented students didn't hand anything in. They were talented, after all. Why bother? The best mark went to the student who I thought didn't have talent. Showing up, even when you know you might not have it, is more than talent. That's a middle finger. I had only admiration and awe for that student. I learned, when you write, someone somewhere is always going to tell you you are not good. Another writer or someone you love or your own self will do that. It takes hard work to not believe that. And talent too.

What's something nobody asks you?

Brand: They never ask about the shape of the poems. So strange, because I am always working with a shape, a method. They say, "she works in the long poem"—well what the heck is that except length? But inside this "long poem," what else? Each step? The lines, the enjambment, et cetera.

Thammavongsa: A shape feels like a minimal concern but is not. Shape is movement, your tinkers and your knots and turns, your fun, how you sustain or build or break sound. How you go. Like dancing. None of that can happen if you haven't a shape or method. It's everything, everything!

They never ask me if my poem about the snow is true. It does not matter if it is true. People want to know if poems about my family are true even though being true is not a matter. I use the chance to talk about my family and memories but what I'm actually doing is talking about craft and how the truth is in that.

Brand: What place/situation/image do you dream about the most?

Thammavongsa: I dream about my family a lot, and dead people I knew as a child. In some strange way I see a connection because my family—which was together when I was a child—is no longer. Divorce. No one knows our love except us. I also dream that I am not dreaming. And that scares me.

Brand: I dream of not being able to speak, or of accidents; just this morning I woke up, thankfully, from a major traffic accident.

What letter of the alphabet do you find complete as a sign of everything?

Thammavongsa: *O.* However it is used, it is never silent. It's a letter that demands to be heard, to be a voice. It's the opening of a mouth, the sound of surprise and pleasure and pain. When you write it out by hand, I love how it feels to make that letter. You begin in one place and you circle around to it, like life. It marks an outside and an inside. And you get to decide where that is. It means what it says. It's so matter-of-fact—upper case or lower case, it's the same. It also looks like a number. Even its value of being nothing is something. That's a sign of everything. Everything in the universe has this shape.

Brand: I think the letter *s.* Sibilant and lucid. In a strange way it does not begin or end and it can undulate into a straight line if it wanted which would make it infinite. It is like a bit of thread and two dunes and two valleys. Then the sound of it echoing but like a sharp dagger or the resonance of water. In this way *s* is treacherous and supine at the same time.

What was the first letter (correspondence) you wrote, to whom and why?

Thammavongsa: Jesus.

Brand: What did it say?

Thammavongsa: It was Christmas. It said, "Happy Birthday." I must have been seven or so. I made a tiny present. I can't remember what it was but I wrapped it up and left it outside on the ground. It disappeared the next day and I thought it had been received. I told my father about it and he told me he thought it was garbage and threw it away. Maybe that is not a real letter. I did not expect to receive a response and I did not use a stamp and envelope. Santa Claus, then. I sent it in the mail. I knew he wasn't real but I wanted to write him. I wanted to take up the space and time of someone who knew the truth of it all and still kept up this appearance.

Brand: I can't remember the first letter I wrote. It was one of two situations though—either a letter dictated by my grandmother to her two daughters in England, my mother and my aunt, or a letter to my grandmother as an exercise in letter writing at school. I suspect the latter since, because of age in my family, I was low on the hierarchy of dictation-takers for my grandmother. In primary school we all learned the formal opening of any letter: "Dear Mrs. Mr. or Miss X, Hope you are well and enjoying the best of health. I write in order to..."

Which contemporary artist interests you?

Thammavongsa: David Hammons. He made snowballs of various sizes and sold them in the streets of New York. By the time the day ended, you couldn't tell anyone what you bought or why it mattered to you and you had nothing to show for it. It didn't mean what you had wasn't real.

Brand: For me, there are two. Torkwase Dyson, her abstract pieces feel alive and moving or as if they are people moving around a room. Josephine Turalba, who makes art—shoes, garments, et cetera—out of war implements like bullets. She collapses the aesthetics of our time into those pieces.

What is the best present you ever received? Why?

Thammavongsa: A pen. It was fancy. It was given to me by someone famous. Whatever I wrote with it looked so beautiful. And maybe it was not so much the pen, but the act by this person that made the gift so special. Like if she picked up a twig and gave it to me, I would have been happy about that too.

Brand: A friend, Angela, went to Havana. In a small book shop she found a 1955 edition of *Canto General* published in Buenos Aires by Editorial Losada, S.A. Absolute best present. She is the kind of friend who knows what you need.

Thammavongsa: That is the best kind of friend. The one who knows what you need.

How about a bad present? Is there such thing? And if there is, what was it for you?

Brand: A bad present would be anything other than a pen, like you, or a book.

What is the worst job you've had?

Thammavongsa: No such thing as a worst job. A job is a job. Something you can do in the world or have to do. I have loved all my jobs. It's the people I worked with. I didn't always like them all.

Brand: Agreed. Yet I think there are bad jobs. Jobs where you are not paid what your labour and life require; jobs where bosses take out of you more than your labour, namely your dignity; jobs where there is also a social requirement for some kind of demeaning act. I never lasted in these jobs.

Thammavongsa: I have had all these jobs, but I always knew I would get out. I saw an end point, and maybe knowing or having that, I did not feel they were bad to me. I worked there or I did that because I wanted to write. And anything I did that gave me that, I could tolerate. But I think about those who do not have that to get to. For them, they are always there, over and over. Lasting.

How about the best? The best job you've had?

Brand: The best job is this one. Or operator at the telephone company when I was in my twenties.

Thammavongsa: The telephone company. Say more.

Brand: The camaraderie. I used to work the night shift—arrive at 7 p.m., leave at 2 a.m., or 3 p.m. to 11 p.m. Mostly other women working there as operators. Then there was also the intimacy of the conversations on the lines, the long distances people called to have crucial, private conversations. There were several banks of stations with plugs and we were all sitting connecting people to other people, and you weren't supposed to but I periodically listened in if I were caught by some urgency in the voice asking me, the long-distance operator, to connect them to someone in Bangkok or Glasgow or Venezuela. Even if I did not understand the language it was wonderful to listen. I remember the evenings vividly. It was never boring. I shouldn't have left that job. But of course that way of communicating has been superseded by new technology. I imagine now it must be the same for say, whoever listens in on us at Skype or Whatsapp or…

Thammavongsa: I love being a tax preparer. Anyone who comes to me knows what I do is valuable. Instantly. There is no explaining why. No waiting around to be noticed. In fact, they line up and are upset when I can't see them. They know I am good.

Brand: Well anyone reading your poetry knows that too. We met, you and I, in poetry. What an ordinary and strange place to meet. We didn't meet on a dance floor or in a factory or in a store or in a line waiting for a bus, but in the structure of nothing, of ambiguity and of malleability, of air and sound. I find that amazing.

Thammavongsa: Like someone working to connect people to other people and then listening in, caught by some urgency in the voice asking.

ANIMATING THEIR WORDS:

Marilyn Dumont and Katherena Vermette

Katherena Vermette: Hello! I hope you are doing well.

I am sending this first note to you while I am thinking of it—which is the only way I can do things these days. My life has had a few changes since I saw you last. The most important is my new daughter, Ruby. She's six weeks old! I am slowly getting out of that stoned baby bubble. I love the baby part, but I am trying to keep working and it's a challenge. There are so many things I really want to do. My partner is taking the year off so he's at home to help, and that really helps. I'm getting back to it and so glad to do this with you!

Not to be like *that*, but *A Really Good Brown Girl* was probably the single most influential book for me as a wannabe poet. In that work, I not only saw much of myself for one of the first times, but you told a story in poetry in a way I had never seen before. I have since learned this is a very Indigenous approach to poetry, drawn from the legacy of oral storytelling, I think. So I have never asked you this before, but why poetry? Why did you choose to tell that particular story in poetry rather than another way?

Marilyn Dumont: Wonderful to correspond with you and congratulations on a new member of the family. How exciting. I think of women with children and, correspondingly, those without children like myself who can't imagine what life would be like having the tremendous responsibility that children bring. I don't know how you get any work done.

I don't feel I necessarily chose poetry as much as it gradually revealed itself to me over many, many years. It began in my early teens. I had questions and no one I know could answer them. I didn't know how to ask them, but poetry communicated to me in an urgent, life-saving way. When I read Middle Eastern poets like Rumi, Rabindranath Tagore, et cetera, I knew there were humans in the world who experienced questions and the human condition in a way that felt familiar. If I couldn't find Indigenous writers to read and reflect on my life, the closest were writers like this. I even quit high school after reading *Education and the Significance of Life* by Jiddu Krishnamurti, who regarded life and others in a way that I could recognize from my own Indigenous life of growing up on the land in part Cree language, part English language.

My family was the typical, big, half-breed clan of ten kids: lots of aunties, uncles and cousins who played guitar, sang and danced. So, the carefully placed words on the page by poets started the journey, but so did dance. I have always been drawn to rhythm because my mother loved to dance and was good at it. So cadence, rhythm, patterns of movement always struck me deeply as shaping life in ways that are powerful but often undervalued or unrecognized. I see this energy in dance, in drumming, in any repetitive motion that creates energy which can be passed on to others. My other influence is music. I secretly wanted to be a singer or dancer, and both these desires arise in poetry for me.

Another influence was hearing and watching Indigenous orators/speakers over the years. The people I was listening to ranged from brothers, sisters and cousins, to more famous people like John Tootoosis Senior who spoke at a University of Calgary Aboriginal student organization in the eighties. I recognized that they possessed an oratory skill that involves a lot more than the voice in the presentation of a story, and I watched how they animated their words.

The other reason poetry became my form, or seemed to fit, was because poets are subversive. They subvert language and, within that, thought and perception. I am still finding new ways in which I am drawn to poetry.

Vermette: I love what you say here. You are so quotable! I relate to these ideas of poetry as revealing and having urgency. I am looking up Krishnamurti now. Sounds in line with a lot of yogic reading and study I've been doing lately. Thanks muchly!

I am glad you mentioned music. I think music is integral to poetry and not mentioned enough. I too would have been a musician. If I could sing, that's what I'd do. All the time. In my childhood, it was more of a Steppenwolf (father) and Johnny Cash (mother) situation, so this is what I took with me. Music has a way of accessing emotional response so quickly. It has everything— tones and rhythms and words too! I immediately try and learn the lyrics of songs and see what they mean.

My family hates it, but most of the time I can't have music in the background. I am too distracted by what they are saying or what the rhythm is doing. I am super picky and need music to go with want I am thinking or doing, like violin concertos for long drives, or Ani DiFranco for big cleaning. I use it to get me in the creative zone and curate different playlists for different projects, and it has to be just right. Do you know about this theory that minor notes make you sad and major notes make you happy? I just learned this. It felt like the best kind of truth. My partner is a musician and watching him write songs taught me a lot about my poetry process. For him, it's about the melody first, then he finds lyrics to fit into that. For me, it's the opposite; I find a word or phrase, and then another, and use the words to figure out what the poem is going to sound like and make its rhythm.

AN OTHER STORY
Katherena Vermette

this country has an other story
one that is not his
or hers
or ours

it is written
in water
carved on earth
every stone
a song
that echoes
the erosion
hold one
to your ear
whispers
rise

this country has another story
and it is not his
or hers
or even ours

it is scrolled on wind
painted in blood
every bone
sings
hold them
to your heart
those buried voices
still
rise

Dumont: I guess I ask you a question now. How do you manage writing and parenting? What relationship do you see between the two?

Vermette: I don't know. My eldest is eighteen this year so I've been a parent for a while. I have written ever since I could but really started thinking of it as a vocation and a craft when my children were small, so in many ways my growing as a writer has directly corresponded with their growing up. If I think about it, they are probably my primary audience. When I started writing about my childhood it was because I wanted to know and remember everything for myself and for them. I didn't want them to grow up like I did, but I still wanted them to learn from it, as I did.

When I think about what I write and why, I think of big, important words like *truth* and *beauty*. This is what I strive for, even if I don't always get there. I want to write the truth, even when it looks ugly and I want to find the beauty in it—which is the real truth—that there is beauty in everything. Underneath my sarcasm and die-hard realism—that is to say my depressing melodrama—I am an optimist. I have tried to write this and have tried to show this to my girls, too.

At its core, or at its beginning, my writing is about making sense of my world. I am slow to respond to things and like to ponder for a long time, so writing becomes an extension of this thinking. Sometimes I don't know what I think until I write it down, or until I read what I wrote. In a practical way, being a parent gives me lots of time to think, from driving my kids around (endlessly) to hours spent breastfeeding (also endless), I can mull through quite a bit. I also like a little chaos and often need the drama of pushing up against a deadline to get things done. I seem to never have any time to actually write, only to think about writing. Parenting is all about these things: drama and chaos with long stretches doing things you want to do, just not for as long as you're stuck doing them.

Meaty thoughts on a Tuesday morning! Where to go from here? Process? I am constantly thinking about process and how important it is. What's yours?

Dumont: Process, hmm. Like you, I never have time for my own creation with full-time teaching now, but my process is long and slow. Right now, I have been looking at a quote from a marvellous book of poetry, which won the Pulitzer in 2016, entitled *Olio* by Tyehimba Jess. "We've mostly owned our songs more than ourselves," he writes in "Jubilee Mission." There's something I want to respond to in this quotation. This is my process: a long slow reflection on something as though it's a living thing growing inside me, until I work through it on paper. So the writing process is fascinating to me, how words enter us and settle in us, how we digest them and eventually something emerges, often something as surprising and mysterious as the process which began the musing.

What you have written about parenting and writing makes sense to me and as someone who lives and works alone, reflecting on your experience of writing is so holistic in terms of your relationships with others that it seems like such a richer process because it involves your children.

I want to ask you if you think our literature is becoming more recognized, and if so why do you think that is? It's a very different writing climate from when I began publishing in the eighties. It now doesn't feel as odd, marginal, exotic or as lonely as it once did. Your thoughts?

Vermette: There is a fast/slow to poetry, isn't there? A long gestation and an unpredictable birth. It is urgent and it does grow. It can come out fast and hard, or painfully slow. I have learned to be relaxed about the process. I used to have to scurry away to my notebook whenever something came, certain it would fly away if I didn't catch it. Now I let the anxiety ease and trust that it'll come when I can write it. Catherine Hunter taught me that. She was one of my first university poetry teachers, and once I had lost a bunch of poems on a dead computer. I was heartbroken thinking they were gone forever, but she was like, "They came from you so they are still inside you." So I relaxed and recreated them. I haven't been anxious about losing anything again.

Why is our writing so hot right now, hey? I am of two minds on this one. On one hand I think we've always had a bunch of fierce warrior writers who have worked their asses off and created. We who are writing now are just the next wave. But I also think there is a certain amount of trendiness these days, something about the reconciliation (trademark® to Canada) that has lent to a surge of attention. But that has nothing to do with us, really. Many people are interested in our stories and that's great—Indigenous folks want Indigenous lit because we want to finally see ourselves in these books or learn more about our nation or nations like ours, and non-Indigenous folks are interested because, well, maybe it's a trend or maybe its time has just come. I have had many long and hard conversations about cultural appropriation this past year and I think it comes down to authenticity. So many people want authentic stories, whether it's from someone like them or someone different.

You wanna talk about cultural appropriation? It feels like a can of worms but could be fun.

Dumont: Sure let's talk about cultural appropriation. The other issue that has emerged for me is the concept of Indigenous stories being healing; however, surely Indigenous writers can write stories that don't heal. What about a writer who employs story to self-aggrandize their writing and not the community? The two may be related if we think of the recent case of Jospeh Boyden.

What are your thoughts?

Vermette: A friend of mine, who is a cultural teacher and community organizer, told me once that stories need to show a way out, that it's irresponsible to tell a sad story without also telling how to heal from it. She was thinking of the youth she works with and the epidemics of suicide, violence and drugs, and felt that Indigenous stories needed to rise above the "poverty porn."

I think about this often when I write. I think about the responsibility we have to young people and the communities we write about but I don't think this means we can't talk about the hard stuff, or that we have to be preachy or didactic in this idea of healing. I think the act of writing and giving voice is an act of healing on its own.

But I'm talking about truthful stories. When someone tells a story out of pity or misunderstanding, that is not healing. That's insulting. When someone tries to speak for someone else, that is an act of abuse. When someone pretends to be someone they are not, they are living a lie. If someone is living a lie, how can they tell the truth? My understanding of stories and storytelling is that they should strive to be truthful above all else. I include poetry in this, of course.

But I give this question back to you as well. What do you think?

Dumont: I agree very much with your points. I think one of the differences between Indigenous storytelling and some of the contemporary English canon is that Indigenous storytelling is intimately connected with identity/territory/kinship which is different from narrative components in Euro-Western culture where story is often about authorial licence/individualism/the esteemed role of the artist—artists being inspired by the gods. I am grateful to come from the tradition of Indigenous storytelling.

In my poetry, I am influenced by the voices that have taught me the beauty of Indigenous ways by orators as well as the Indigenous writers who came before me.

I COME SOUNDING AFTER
Marilyn Dumont

Nista mina   Nista mina   Nista mina
Stamina
Nista mina

sweet syllables recalled
summoned from a dormant motherly shoot
ripening its way to my
larynx strung to my sound-belly
aural memory loosening

a sound root
stretched over dusty tongue and ear

pull together   no sound alone
union of larynx and lips
sounding our nehiyawak-bodysong
through our moose stew and bangs
our dry meat and baked bannock
our bone marrow soup

I come sounding after
Nikawiy, Nohtawiy
and some swimming of a brother's laugh splashing my face

I come sounding after
Nimooshom
Nokom

nista mina

nimiton
mistikwan

this tongue loosens, delights
lights   enlightens
aural memory arriving home
from a long time ago:
nikawiy, thank you for birthing me,
nohtawiy , thank you for never leaving me

a sound alone

Nista mina comes from you both
recalling sound sliver
nista mina my mother combs my hair,
my father tickles my feet,

nista mina, my brother teases me,
nista mina they call me back through kin vibrations
faces envelope me in the electric energy of affinity
opening the front door
pitikwe

I am a ventriloquist of my parents, nokom, nimooshom

my lips, tongue, larynx
thread sound of the same mother tongue
stringing nista to mina

I'm tired
Nista mina

I'm hungry
Nista mina

I am lonely for your sounds

Nista mina

Nista mina   me too
Nehiyawak   Cree language
Nikawiy   mother
Nohtawiy   father
Nimooshom   grandfather
Nokom   grandmother
Nimiton   my mouth
Mistikwan   my head
Pitikwe   come in

Vermette: It's been a tough (understatement) time for Indigenous justice (or lack thereof) with both George Stanley's acquittal in the death of Colten

Boushie and Raymond Cormier's acquittal in the death of Tina Fontaine. How important do you think the politics/issues/bullshit are to your work?

Dumont: Indigenous justice or injustice is omnipresent. Throughout the history of Indigenous peoples on their homeland, injustice is pervasive, so it seems it doesn't really matter what era, place, I write about—it's present. It does inform my work; even when I'm not citing something specific, it haunts it.

Presently, I am slowly (snail's pace) working on poetry about Amiskwaci-washigan, and it's embedded in the land, so it's ever-present.

What about you? How important is it to your work?

Vermette: I like your description of its hauntingness. It's true. It's always there. I want to write only about beauty and strength, and I can always find that, but it's not the whole story. There is always tragedy. There's always something that could have been different "if only." I don't know why I don't just let myself rage. Maybe I'm afraid I'll never stop.

I'm curious about your new stuff. Do you want to talk about it more? It's okay if you don't, of course. I found that *The Pemmican Eaters* was also integrally tied to land as well as history and the present day. How do you do that? Is it a conscious choice?

Dumont: I am working toward a collection about the Indigenous history of Edmonton. I am approaching it by reading as much of the history as I can from both settler and Indigenous perspectives. While reading settler history, Indigenous history is often found by reading between the lines. For example, in historical accounts of "explorers" like Anthony Henday there are mentions of Indigenous peoples travelling with them on expeditions, which is expected, but when the number of Indigenous peoples is actually revealed one realizes that their numbers indicate how much the Indigenous guides, interpreters, hunters, labourers, et cetera, contributed to the "explorations," so that the project would have not been possible without them; however, they are only mentioned in passing. Similar kinds of support in surviving were extended to the immigrant farmers that populated the prairies. Without Indigenous support, many of these people would have died.

One of the surprising things I have learned doing this historical research is that my mother's family (Dufresnes) was connected to the fur-trading clerk class. Francois Dufresne, my great-grandfather, was the illegitimate son of Chief Factor Rowand, who was the HBC factor in Edmonton and one of the most powerful HBC factors on the prairies. So, essentially, Chief Factor Rowand is then my great-great-grandfather. All of this has paused my writing as I digest how to write about this in my collection. I find it humorous and quite typical of Indigenous-settler relations.

AN ACQUIESCENCE TO NOT KNOWING:

Sue Goyette and Linda Besner

Sue Goyette: Hi, Linda. I'm enthralled by *Feel Happier in Nine Seconds*. There's such complexity and fluidity at once *and* it's hilarious. I've read it once and am going to read it again, slower. I raced through it in that first-read joy!

Linda Besner: Hi, Sue. Thanks so much for the kind words—that's so nice to hear. I've read both your most recent, *Penelope in the First Person*, and your first book, *The True Names of Birds*. I found both had such an active intelligence and willingness to push the line. I would love to talk about long lines and how a line finds its shape.

But also, perhaps an even more urgent question that needs to be addressed immediately: *What* is happening with that epic plant on your Facebook?

Goyette: Ha! It's an agave. It's thirty to thirty-five years old and is about to flower for the first and only time and then the plant will die. It feels too monumental, too unbelievable not to honour it so I visit it every day in the public gardens and then post a photo of the progress. It definitely feels like a feminist manifesto or something. Wild, eh?

Besner: That's amazing. Whenever it crosses my feed there's something about the juxtaposition of the agave photos you post with quotes from women like Alison Bechdel, Lady Gaga, Audre Lorde, Lucille Ball and Janelle Monae with this image that's half-beautiful, half-ludicrous—that plant is phallic as hell! I've been wondering what you were saying with it. It seemed to me like sort of a comment on how singular and sort of ugly and misshapen sexuality and power are. Like at first glance it seems as if it should be a serene post—a plant and an inspirational quote from a well-known woman—but then the plant itself is so shocking in its determination it makes you look at the quote again.

Goyette: It is phallic as hell, or something as hell, eh? I've been thinking about shame and vulnerability a lot. Also how we engage with the private and public aspects of our lives. Here's this plant, manifesting itself into flower with the shape that it is and having no choice but to continue in the middle of the city. It's so interesting how its form, her form, has yet to be fully realized and how we have all these feelings when we look at her. I have a lot of conversations in the garden, mostly with women, about that. How I can relate to this process somehow. How we lose form to find form. As for the quotes, I choose them on the day, intuitively. I do have some saved but mostly I come across something that fits.

How was it for you when you were writing the sections "ROYGBP, or, Recital of Your Gently Burning Perfections" and "Magnetic Variations on One and Six" in *Feel Happier*? Both those sections share a complexity, a cohesion and a structure or design that deepens the complexity. "Magnetic Variations" is spectacular, an expansive eruption of idea/word/colour/velocity. I can easily imagine the section performed somehow and it would be fabulous. How did you approach and find your way in?

BELLS, LIBERTY, UNDUE EXULTATION
Linda Besner

I blew a baleful valentine to Napoleon in Elba:
what with your bullrush libido, and the bleary

albatross latched to my earlobe, life in *la ligne aérienne*
is coming unglued. All my unbillable hours delivering boiled waterlilies

in a wheelbarrow; it's enough to give Lillian Hellman
the collywobbles. I lost a castle, a thimble, I clung

to a mineral libretto, I'm drinking for two. My blood is leaky, blustery,
    it billows
with lamblike culpability, it's richer than you. My celebrity

is the empty cymbal in an all-white school band. Listen,
I'm the club soda you spilled through the crack in freedom's

umbrella. I'm the eel-ribboned Easter hat with Belarusian diamonds.
Listen, you won't believe who's back:

my flibbertigibbet hymen. A clang from the *cloche* tolling
the closing of Heaven's last hyperlink.

Besner: I really love what you say about how the agave has no choice—it doesn't get to decide when or where to show itself, and its inner life is literally bursting its skin—there's definitely going to be a display, and the plant doesn't have any control over who's there to see it.

"Magnetic Variations" came out of a study I read about synaesthesia. Usually people with grapheme-colour synaesthesia have different associations—my *b* is yellow, but your *b* is green. These researchers found a bunch of people who had identical associations, and they cross-referenced the letter-colour pairings with those Fisher Price fridge magnet letters from the seventies and eighties. Identical! It showed that synaesthetic associations can be learned. I got obsessed with this study and spent quite a long time playing around with the letter sets it created. I grouped the red letters together and the orange letters together, et cetera, and tried to use them for things. You can make a lot of words with the red set—it's AGSMY, so you can make SAG and GAS and MAGMA and so on. But some of them are annoyingly impossible! The green set is DJPV and you can't do anything with that. After much trial and error, I settled on the pattern that's in the book, which is also quite complicated to explain and I am 90 percent sure people don't get it, even after they read the rather complicated note I put in the back.

Point being, for me "Magnetic Variations" took on this trippy, semi-mystical quality where I felt like I was staring down into the very atoms of language: the alphabet itself was streaming past me all Starship Enterprise, these smallest units of meaning sort of parting to let me through. I worked it all up with markers—I went through several boxes of Crayola—and I've never felt more shocked by what I was doing. The physical process was so odd. I got really good at holding all the markers, uncapped, in between the different fingers of my left hand and plucking out the one I needed, drawing the letter and replacing it while plucking out the next. It was like embroidery or weaving… maybe it wasn't, I don't know how to do either of those things. But the extreme tactility of the process made the alphabet feel like a physical material I was using, and the brightness of the colours on the page, the juiciness of the markers… I had a whole feeling of God creating light and also creating the word, and the word and light being the same thing, and here with the coloured letters I felt like I saw what that meant: the different letters were literally different wavelengths of light.

And then the weird unfitness of it sometimes, too—there were letters that I would get wrong over and over because they just didn't *feel* like that colour to me. *D* is green according to the Fisher Price schema, but I felt so strongly that *D* should be orange! And I was always getting *F* and *V* mixed up—*F* is supposed to be purple and *V* green, but to me it should be the opposite. I think there's some interference from "violette" and "vert"—and maybe "leaf" and "feuille" as well. *F* and *V* actually sound very similar; it's weird that purple and green look pretty different.

Can I ask a different question about *Penelope*? As I kept coming across one of the repeated phrases—"I dress dutifully"—I started thinking about what duty means and how it sounds like such an old-fashioned notion that doesn't get a lot of press these days. And then I was thinking about getting dressed and what it means to be dutiful about that, and it made me think both of convention and modesty, but also of the duty to be fashionable: to stay relevant, to keep up with the times. I wanted to ask both about what duty means to you and also what duty in the poetic sense means to you. I've only recently become aware that poetry, like everything else, has trends. I don't think I really understood that other things had trends either, actually—like history or politics or intellectual life. How shaped do you feel you are by these external forces?

Goyette: Watching the agave has been so evocative for me for how the experience or progression it's making is so kin to everything. Poetry, for example;

how I turn up and go along with the going along, if that makes sense. And like the agave, that creative act can then become public and if it does I have no control over who is going to see/read/hear it and how they're going to respond. So it's a master class in not knowing what I'm doing and doing it nonetheless. Vulnerability, maybe. And, weirdly or more vulnerably, shame. Is it the way I'm wired? Is it how I approach my vocation? Is it a combination of both? I mostly have no idea.

I really love that you were willing to go along with the "trippy, semi-mystical quality" the work invited you to engage with. That seems key to my practice as well, an acquiescence to not knowing, feeling the force of the work's current and serving it as best as I can. I find that particular vulnerability terrifying when I can't tell if it's working or if it's going to turn into one hot, galactic mess but the process is so invigorating, so compelling that it feels worth the risk. It's definitely a groove that I don't always connect with.

In some ways, when I'm engaging with my work this way, I am thinking very much of duty, of the poetic duty that you mentioned. For me, that sense of duty (which feels like it comes from maybe the practice or exertion of cultural norms and what is considered okay or acceptable and, in turn, gives me a sense of safety, a sense of fitting in if I comply) is something I have to fight or disrupt continually though it's an ancient need in me: to fit in, to be liked. And what may even be trickier to deal with is how I perpetuate or regulate that duty in myself, inherently, without knowing that I'm doing it; how I have internalized that sense of duty without challenging it, by the spoonful of mainstream media, of advertising, of big and unchallenged beliefs about gender and agency that I've grown up with; and how I edit myself so I don't go too far, or too wild, too big; the ways I keep myself legible and ultimately "safe." One of the challenges—word by word—for me is reaching into new territory rather than circling and heading back to territory I am more comfortable with. Thinking about it now, this practice gives me a new, wilder version of the idea of poetic duty, or maybe the word *duty* now migrates to poetic *integrity* which is what I'd consider a practice of reaching and of risk (and how it constantly terrifies me). I'm really interested in this relationship with duty. What a great question you asked! How about you? Do you reckon with any of this? How do you keep yourself moving into new territory in your work?

Besner: "That particular vulnerability... when I can't tell if it's working or if it's going to turn into one hot, galactic mess"—this is something I really wonder about. What stylistic pitfalls are you most afraid of? What makes you wince when you reread your drafts and then steer in a different direction? And do you trust this wincing?

I definitely feel fearful in my work. But I'm a bit confused about what I'm afraid of and whether that fear is useful or not. I mean, presumably it is both. I feel like the aesthetic I've been most influenced by is sort of cerebral—my writing group (now on a bit of a hiatus) definitely prizes surprise and wordplay and smarty-pants things like that over sincerity or emotional expression— which has mostly been right for me. I don't think I would be happy in an environment that was too touchy-feely in that way. But lately I have been wondering if this is something I want to open the door to a little bit more. In my personal life I am pretty emotive (one friend said to me, "at first if you started crying I thought it was a major crisis but now I'm like: another day at the office") but I haven't been so interested in doing that in my work. I guess—this feels like a very heretical thing to say—I actually don't find, as a reader, that poetry is the best vehicle for conveying emotions. When I read a novel full of feeling, I am very affected by it because the emotions are grounded in character and situation—there are people for me to relate to. In poems, this isn't my experience for the most part. You have such a brief space in which to know the speaker, and the speaker is often very veiled or very exposed. Maybe because it takes me a while to get to know people, I don't have time in the space of a poem to feel like I know the speaker well enough to really share their concerns. Or maybe it's because I go to poetry for an engagement with language itself rather than with people?

I worry about a) repeating myself, and b) *not* repeating myself. In terms of form, I think that means that I feel like I don't want to use an invented form again, even if the first one seemed good and I am still interested in the form; but also, I'm worried about flitting from shiny new thing to shiny new thing and never actually achieving any kind of mastery. What if I just worked in one form my whole life and really learned it? There's something so attractive to me about that kind of discipline, and imagine what you could learn! It really would be a new way of seeing inside how language works. But I think I am maybe a dilettante at heart. In my day job I write non-fiction magazine pieces and what I love and hate about it is that you are always under pressure to quickly learn a whole bunch of new things. Because I'm a general interest writer, I skip around a lot and don't really have an area. I get confused about the utility of such a life—breadth versus depth—when it comes to any kind of knowledge or life experience. I like to learn, but I sometimes wonder if I have the patience to really know anything.

I actually noticed an interesting echo of this "learning" versus "knowing" thing in comparing *The True Names of Birds* to *Penelope*. In *Penelope*, the refrain is of "If I know": "If I know anything, it's about loss"; "if I know aging, / it too is about loss"—but in the poem "Of the Crows that Follow Me" in *The True Names of Birds*, there's a line, "If I've learned anything from him, it's the architecture of isolation." Does this learning-knowing divide speak to you? Seems like Penelope is asserting that she knows things but also troubling that notion by putting the conditional at the fore.

Yeah, I guess duty for me is complicated—in a weird, probably sad way, I like the idea of having duties because I like the idea of someone needing me. I know a lot of people hate obligations, but I kind of love them! I like there to be things that anchor me to the world, I guess. I don't feel like the danger for me is in being too constrained; it's in being too untethered and alone.

In poetic terms, I think I always feel bad that I'm not doing my duty though—not reading enough or the right things, or maybe reading them and secretly not liking them/getting them when it seems like everyone else does. I guess I feel like it's my duty to be open to takes on poetry that don't echo my own—uses I don't use it for, feelings I don't get out of it. When other people like something I don't, I definitely wonder what is wrong with me and want to work harder to see whatever people are seeing. When I fail to love things, I feel like I am failing to do my duty. And I fail to love so many poems! I sometimes wonder if I like poetry at all. Oh god! But I think I also don't completely love most novels I read or music I hear. I think I love visual art best because I don't understand it at all so my critical mind doesn't ruin my pleasure in it.

Goyette: I've been reading a lot of feminist theory these last few months and have been struck by how emotional I feel in the presence of the speculative reach rigorous thinking instigates. It's a cognitive cathedral, orchestral, which is intriguing. Maybe because I'm wired to feel alert in new territory, all of me engages: my brain, my gut and my feelings when I read. Or maybe that's just how I engage or agree to engage with most things. I'm a little operatic. I also experience an emotionality in the company of dry, overly formal and redundant writing which, essentially, can be boiled down to dread. A *put a fork in me, I'm done* dread. This dread, I think, is what I'm afraid of contributing to. And that dread, for me, is when I become more centred in my work than the force of its making, if that makes sense. When I shift from exploratory and alert and game to a more closed system of navigation, for example when I know what's going to happen and where I'm heading is a foregone conclusion, or when I switch to a safer version and the circuitry is closed, then the air becomes stale and the writing feels primarily like a platform for me to say something the way I think it needs to be said. This instigates dread in me. I'm much more entranced by the practice of not knowing and of ongoing meaning-making and engagement, and the contraptions that are left in the wake of that kind of practice. So I guess the stylistic pitfall I'm most afraid of is me thinking and sounding like I know what I'm doing. That seriously makes me fraught with dread.

There are a great many species of winces I experience when I'm done writing something. One of the challenges is to differentiate the wince. Is it just my old wince, the inherent and benign shame that I think I can make something? Or is it the wince of getting a glimpse of where I patched or skidded over something valuable? That wince is constructive, the old, benign wince is like having a limp, something I've gotten used to and generally try to acknowledge and then shelve. There's only so much I can know and do to my writing before it needs a bigger ecosystem to live in. This could mean I send it to someone I trust to tell me if my skirt is in my tights, or I include it in a reading when I get the chance. I'm not so much interested in knowing if people like it or not, it's more about the moment it's received. Readings are good for this; I know in that instant by the silence, the quality of the listening, if there's something worthwhile or not happening. For me, it's not about comprehension but engagement. Then once it's done, it's out of my hands. Then I'm left with that vulnerability/fear and the best I can do is choose to get back to work or not. I've been taking breaks in a way I hadn't before and claiming some time not to write is a new luxury. Which isn't to say that I constantly wrote before, just that the times I wasn't were polluted with regret/remorse/guilt/whatever, and now they're not.

I've been thinking about what you said about form and the need for order in the WTF company of life. And, how, in that way, form invites or gives the wild, the WTF, some space in a poem so that it can then be looked at up close. Has that been your experience?

The dilemma of not being able to do it all the ways is something I can commiserate with. I do think one of the key components to my operating system is learning, which I think is tied to not knowing and being curious. It's interesting that you've tied that learning/knowing to *Penelope* and a poem from *The True Names of Birds* (which was published twenty (!!) years ago). Key to *Penelope* is what you mentioned above about the WTF aspect of life and, I think, when I was writing it, dealing with that exact thing was crucial and her knowing, in this way, was more a posturing in the middle of a serious WTF couple of decades rather than her actually knowing something. It was her way of asserting some kind of agency to the situation, I think. The "architecture of isolation" is a little wince-y for me in the way seeing a photo of myself in junior high would be... As in, *egads*.

EXCERPT FROM *PENELOPE*
Sue Goyette

The weeks wake to more months. Years. Can we get another table
in the beer tent? I'm asked. There's a beer tent? I reply. I'm flustered.

And I'm drunk. The visitors are potent compliments. They've never seen
a better spoon, tasted better brew. Our harbour, according to them,

is the finest they've laid eyes on. Each stone in its proper
place, how had I come up with that? My cup is kept proficiently

filled. And my tongue rallies back. I banter, I cajole. I screech
the crooked logic women know when our hearts are aghast and silenced.

I tend to the visitors with appalling decorum. They cheer me on,
so I blow. I blow. Odysseus' candle sputters then quits. I did that.

Besner: I know what you mean about the closed-off quality of work that sounds like all the thinking and feeling happened before the poem was actually written—like the space the poem actually occupies is a sort of aftermath rather than traces of the struggle still existing in the mental atmosphere of the poem. I like to be able to see the poet thinking.

And yeah, the thing of testing things out on audiences I get. It can be help-ful to feel the quality of people's silence as they listen. But personally I am also a bit suspicious of my own reading persona. I worry that I am snake-oiling bad poems to seem good by selling them too well, kind of. Or at least that there are certain qualities that make for poems that work well out loud, and that be-cause I am more likely to get validating audience responses for those kinds of qualities, I end up writing more poems in that vein—poems that are funny or that have dense sound structures. Also, I wonder if the emphasis in the poetry world on reading one's work publicly makes me less likely to explore more personal territory. I don't particularly want to start crying onstage, which is a real concern. It's tricky because I actually love giving readings—I'm lucky that way, I know a lot of writers hate it—but I do feel suspicious that the expect-ation that I'll be the public face of my own work affects what I end up feeling comfortable writing.

I mean, yeah, I guess I think of form as a wild thing—nature is all about symmetry and patterns. I think in the ROYGBP section of *Feel Happier* I was trying to do a bit of a takeoff on the very tight constraints of "Magnetic Variations"—I thought of the letter sets in ROYGBP as notes I would go back to; the home chord, I guess, around which all kinds of other jazzier things could be flying. Wilderness is very structured, that's why when you eliminate a species you fuck everything up. Which is not to say forms are fixed. Finding new forms and structures is also what nature does.

I really want the agave to bloom before our conversation is over!

Goyette: I hear you about being suspicious of your own reading. Reckoning with the performative aspect of reading poems while migrating from private to public is no small thing. I think when I'm reading new work at a reading I'm more alert to how it's making me feel rather than the response the poem's getting. The glare of hearing the words out loud makes the missteps or bull-shittery way more obvious to me. Those moments when I glided or took the easy route, the hollow words, the dramatic words, the *feeling* words that ha-ven't earned their place, the smart sounding words that are barren, the clever assertions, the trussed-up wit. All the times I went for the brandish rather than made room for the poem and for the person encountering the poem are instantly apparent. This listening is apart, for me, from performance. It's more about seeing the poem moving back to the woods and getting a glimpse of it before it disappears.

I'm interested in contributing to a space that is lively and interactive. I love having a conversation that may begin with poetry but manifests into something bigger, something expansive and creative and unexpected. I think a lot about this, what an opportunity it is to be in a room full of people who are all willing to participate and recharge and lean in. Being part of that kind of community seems crucial to me. I also think a lot about poetry readings in general and how they can be curated or hosted to enliven that exchange. Do you go to a lot of readings? What do you like best about them as a member of the audience? What makes a reading meaningful to you?

Personal experience was why I started to write in the first place. I needed to extract a lot of experience in order to transform it into something redeemable, something worthwhile when I was young. Reading saved me and books gave me a sense of belonging that was crucial to my well-being. I'd read stories or poems for their company, for how I could relate and belong to them somehow, for how they afforded my experience some dignity, so my writing started out extremely personal. I think I was redefining or reclaiming my first-person, staking a claim for my version and, in this way, writing saved me. I've had to learn the difference between writing to row myself out of a swamp and being engaged in the vocation, the discipline, the creative act of meaning-making that isn't recollecting but forward moving. When something happens that I need to deconstruct or reconfigure, I write it out, usually adapting a form and treating it like a poem. I've had to learn to distinguish these "poems," which are vital just to me, from the poems that are not so singular or private. Sometimes these personal poems continue to progress until the personal recedes or contributes something but is not the focal point of the poem. In other words, sometimes after I've processed what I needed to of the experience, it becomes part of the ecosystem of my thinking. Does that make sense? In some ways, everything I write is personal but when my loyalty shifts from experience to poem I know I'm done processing and have begun to actually write again.

I really like the stage when I'm alert to writing, when connections start happening, when synchronicity abounds, when I encounter thinking/art/company that sparks. That giddy-up, *yesyesyes* stage when words thrum and lean in together. I don't feel this very often, hardly at all, but when I find myself in the groove there is a flow to my days that I can't instigate or replicate. It's just there. And then it's not. *Don't think about your feet when you dance*—is that a thing? Or just my experience? Either way, once I start thinking, cognitively, about what I'm doing, I'm done for, I get self-conscious, I lurch, I stall.

As for the agave, any day now, I hope. What a slow-cooking adventure! The conversations I have in its proximity are amazing. It seems to percolate the air and invite an opening somehow. And the behind-the-scenes drama is startling! One gardener pronouncing it dead, another scoffing at the idea of it being dead… It's a very public manifestation of something, I just can't tell what that something is yet.

Besner: I definitely go to fewer readings than I used to. I'm not 100 percent sure why. In part, when I moved back to Montreal I found the scene revolved around the universities, so I felt more peripheral. In a way, it was very freeing. Toronto can get overwhelming because you want to support everybody by going to their events, but there are so many writers you inevitably miss some and feel guilty.

I used to feel a stronger sense of community as well—I think in part when my first book came out, coincidentally four or five of my close friends were having their first books out in the same year, so it felt like something we were all doing together. Now I guess my cohort is not so closely in step, so my second book felt a bit lonelier. And all the #MeToo stuff has opened my eyes to how horrible other people's experiences have been in communities I've been a part of, which makes me feel so guilty. I feel very ill-equipped to find the most just and kind way through these painful discussions. I've mostly just been trying to read, listen and talk in person to people close to me. It seems like I've been incredibly lucky in that I got a very ordinary educational experience and have been treated professionally in my relationships with editors and others. I feel weird and stupid for not knowing that this can be legitimately categorized as "lucky;" I thought it was normal. Now I feel a bit paranoid. This sense that participating in professional or personal relationships with people who have harmed others bars injured parties from the community I think I understand, but I find it hard to find a stable set of feelings/practices about it. On an institutional level, I feel like there are some clear things that can be done, like laying out policies and rules, but so much of the literary world is in a nebulous, semi-personal, semi-professional zone that I don't quite know how to navigate other people's relationships with each other. I was brought up to think a) people act horribly and that's just life so my job is to be very wary, and b) people's personal lives are mostly not my business. Now I am trying to move past those ideas but I'm definitely just learning, and currently feel like I'm failing everyone on all sides.

That's so interesting about your process, that germ of feeling or experience that is initially the subject and that recedes as the poem comes into its identity as a poem. I think for me the poem always starts as pure language. Initially, it's not about anything, it's just words drawn together by some kind of magnetic attraction. And then as words start to gather around these energetic nodes, I start to get a sense of what they might be saying. And I guess at that juncture the feelings or experiences I've been turning over in my mind find their way in.

I find dance such an interesting art form in that way—this question of what is happening in your mind, and the distinction between thinking and feeling. I once had an opportunity to interview a researcher who was studying dance and cognition—what role planning plays and how dance pedagogy could be improved. Because I'm attracted to structure, I love formal dance— the patterns you can create. But as a dancer I'm not actually that good at bridging the cognitive tasks of counting and visualizing the next sequence of steps with the abandonment to the moment you need to really feel the movements and give yourself up to the joy of them. I really struggle with metrical arrangements in poetry in a similar way—I'd like to have better control of the metres in my work but I've never really learned to scan properly. I hear stresses everywhere!

Goyette: I really like readings that surprise me, readers who understand how to curate a space, hosts who know how to welcome and initiate that space. I like when there are a variety of things to listen to, when there's a visual component to the night. A mix of poetry, comedy, song, art and then a conversation after the artists have situated themselves in their work. I've also been thinking how it would be great to have the opportunity to hear people read works-in-progress, mid-swim, and listen to what they're thinking about and how. As I said, I really like a good conversation/discussion/Q & A at a reading. Also, wouldn't it be great to hear people read their B-sides? The poems that don't often get read, the ones that have remained silent? Or poems they think don't work?

I've invited other people to read my work when I launched *outskirts*. I think there were thirteen or fifteen people reading and they all got to choose their poem. It was such a great way to launch the book into the community and the audience was a wonderful combination of people who normally wouldn't go to a poetry reading, including my kids! For *The Brief Reincarnation of a Girl* three of my friends and I divided the text into parts and read the whole poem. We invited everyone in the audience to stay silent during the intermission and the energy got really intense, the listening so potent, so active. Another friend directed the lighting so the space collaborated with the text. It was such a great experience.

I do find myself lonely for a poetry community. There are great poets in Nova Scotia and they are good company when we do get together for whatever reason but I don't keep regular enough company with them and, sometimes, I crave that talk, the reading lists, the jokes and the singular complaints only poets understand. I wish I had more time to hang out and more time to write long letters to people. That is another level of company I'd really appreciate, I think.

The #MeToo movement has had such a direct impact on our community in many of the ways you talked about. And it's a proper and timely conversation to have. Power and how it manifests, how it's exerted, how it's presumed, is something we can all relate and listen to, I think. I've seen my share of power imbalance and inappropriate behaviour and I'm relieved that so many people are speaking out. It's no small thing to break that particular silence, wading through the tenacious and inherent shame before breaking that silence is challenging. What I'm seeing/hearing is an equally tenacious response of support for the people who have felt the brunt of encounters with people who have behaved inappropriately, and that's really heartening. I've learned that I am "friends" on social media with people who haven't always acted respectfully and have had to reconsider those friendships when this new information surfaces. I also like the idea of people being accountable and taking responsibility for their behaviour. I like people using their agency and admitting that they have made mistakes and are willing to make amends. I really like when people then do what they say they are going to do. I support that kind of responsibility and exertion. I also respect how the people who have experienced the harm may not be ready to forgive. I respect their anger. The pain, the social discomfort, the awkwardness, is part of moving forward, I think. It's a new vulnerability or maybe an old vulnerability we're reacquainting with publicly.

I'm really interested in how this conversation is moving us forward, though it doesn't always feel like it is moving at all. I am so sorry for anyone who finds themselves in the position of being stuck and in pain and alone. I find myself listening more, not filling the gaps so fast in conversations. That's a thing I can do for someone. Easily.

I'm so intrigued to read about how you think about dance. Pina Bausch is one of the people I'd choose if I could have lunch with anyone. I'd want to hear more about how and what she thinks about in terms of movement, bodies, creation and performance. The request she made to her dancers—*show me what it feels like*—and her use of movement rhymes are things I think about all the time. I had a YouTube clip of one of her dances in a browser tab for over a year and would watch it every day. I still couldn't pull it off but I feel like it's in my bloodstream, that four or whatever minutes of movement and cohesion and sequence and fluency and articulation and whimsy and body-as-contraption. I totally get caught up in the movement, the vitality, and so can't count or even pace sequence when I engage with dance. When I'm watching something by, say, Marie Chouinard my whole body wants to combust, to extol that kind of mobility and stretch and build strength. I watch dance for how it moves to make meaning without verbal articulation. It stretches my imagination, introduces possibilities (both corporeal and cognitive) that I'd have a hard time articulating but know somehow below and beyond words.

I could talk about this forever, movement and cognition and the similarities poetry shares with dance, how words want to break from traditional narrative or linear structure or etymology to make their own singular movement/sequence forward and how watching or engaging with dance strengthens, not necessarily the ability to do that, but the inspiration or the risk it takes to even try. ("I hear stresses everywhere" is such a great line and I can totally relate to it; it makes for such an interesting/engaged reading.)

I'm about to read your first book, *The Id Kid*, and am really looking forward to it. In the meantime, I'm wondering how you feel about it now? I notice there's a few years' gap between books. Was that a conscious choice?

Besner: There's a six-year gap between my two books. Honestly, it was because publishing a book made me feel horrible! I was terribly disappointed in myself for not making it better. I find it so hard to handle the inevitable gap between what you want your work to be and what it is—you just can never quite make the thing you were hoping to make. I've been lucky to get a fair bit of positive critical attention for my work, which does make me feel a bit better, whether or not it should. But I think the sense of failure is just kind of a permanent discontent with the impossibility of leaping out of the world of concrete things. My favourite time in the writing process is what I call the "golden haze"—those times when a poem is just scribbled, disconnected notes that I haven't tried to actually make into a coherent thing yet—it's still a sort of Platonic ideal notion of "poem." The worst time is first typing it up. I work longhand for as long as I possibly can and then type it up when I really need to see line lengths and move things around. That moment when it gets transferred into that colder, dead form is always sort of chilling. I don't feel quite that way about my books—I think the words are still alive in there some-where—but I think it's just the crushing sadness of the loss of the potential that has been traded in for the actual. In the end, I wrote these specific poems and not different ones, and all the possible different choices I could have made have been snipped off and this is what's left, which is never enough.

It's interesting what you said about the luxury of not writing, and especial-ly of not feeling guilty about not writing. Have you ever seriously considered stopping writing altogether? It feels like there's a taboo about doing that—as if once you self-identify as a writer you would be killing yourself off if you stopped being one. Or you'd be letting the team down. You quit on a tiny, struggling club you were once a member of, and now they're going to have trouble making rent on the tiny hall where they have their meetings, and also who will bring the doughnuts now?

Goyette: I like that you know you're a slow writer. Half the battle, it seems, is to figure out what I need and how I am. I'm a fast writer, which means I have tall piles of poems that will never see the light of day. I write a lot when I write and hardly any of it is worthwhile so it takes me awhile to accumulate anything of value.

And I hear you about that gap between the imagined, the genius, the chan-delier of illuminated reach of an idea and then the actual thing. It's like sea-weed, eh? Flexing green and bending in the light and water and then just a heap of clump when it's pulled from it.

I used to break up with my writing all the time. Send it packing. "That's it, we're done," I'd say. Which, I realize now, is like trying to break up with my shadow. It's just how I am. I write. But there are times when I don't write and I've learned to unpollute those times. As for letting down the team, I wish there was a team. I'd love a team. It is indeed a struggling club and we're having trouble making rent and I wish I felt more connected to the people in that metaphor. I'm not sure anyone would notice if I stopped writing, to be honest. Most days, my poetry team is made up of ghosts, which could be me. Maybe I'm a bit of a loner.

Who are you reading/watching/listening to that riles you up in a good way? Who is particularly smoking for you?

Besner: I've been reading a bunch of moral philosophy books recently—Iris Murdoch's *The Sovereignty of Good* (Sue Sinclair's suggestion, actually) and Kwame Anthony Appiah's *The Honor Code: How Moral Revolutions Happen* as well as his *Cosmopolitanism: Ethics in a World of Strangers*. Partly for work—I'm putting together a non-fiction piece about changing notions of "the good"— and partly just because I am super confused about what "the good" is! Ethical questions really exercise me and I'm not at all convinced that I know how to behave ethically.

What about you? What books, music, et cetera, have been shaping your world these days?

Goyette: I'm reading a couple things right now but I'm taking a class so I'm mostly reading texts about gender identity and how the construct of that identity is enforced. On my night table and in my backpack are: Donna J. Haraway's *Staying with the Trouble: Making Kin in the Chthulucene; Wisdom Rising* by Lama Tsultrim Allione; and *Chaos: Making a New Science* by James Gleick. I read these in small doses when I have time. I'm interested in them for how they engage with vulnerability and not-knowingness. This seems crucial right now and I want to know more about staying open and not retreating or disengaging with whatever I'm experiencing, especially when I feel like I have no idea what I'm doing.

Besner: It's so amazing to take classes! I often daydream about going back to school—there's so much I want to learn about. Can you say more about your classes? I think you said earlier you are working on a thesis?

Goyette: I'm in a women and gender studies program so have been essentially studying systems of oppression. It's pedagogically brutal: patriarchy, colonialism, racism, classism, ableism, ageism, neoliberalism, neoconservatism and on it goes, systems that are self-sustaining, have been made culturally normative and performed by all of us. By the end of the last term, I found I could hardly breathe and I now understand that I am someone who needs doses of air to aerate theory, and that being able to meet those needs is a privilege not everyone has. The difference between ideology and experience is something I reckon with all the time. I've learned a great many things. I've mostly learned how little I do know. I can read theory now, I can write discourse about that theory, I can better concentrate and read more critically than I ever have. I have some points of reference that are helpful. I felt like I really needed to overturn my vocabulary, give my thinking some voltage. It was interesting to *feel* myself change, feel my brain become more active. Learning is a tremendous gift; I really love how I feel, how engaged I am when I'm reading work that sings with its exertion and reach, with a rigorous intellect that has found its stride. It's related to reading good poems somehow. But I was mighty creaky when I first started last year and I understand how easy it would be to slide back into that creakiness. And I've certainly been humbled, have made mistakes and have said some genuinely dumb things in the last year, which is another form of learning, I think.

Besner: Before we end, can I ask a craft question about line lengths? How do you know when it's time to break a line? This is something I really struggle with. It puts pressure on my opposing aspirations to be loose and to be neat and tidy.

Goyette: I pay attention to line breaks for the space they provide, the pause, the slack or tension they make, the breath they imply. Each line has its own voltage, its own force. I was recently at this talk where the speaker got us all to chant some words and it's a beautiful thing to join voices in a word. I could hear the lifespan of our breaths, how it took a bit of time for us all to find the sonic groove of the word. And for some seconds our voices were ripe, became singular, before breaking apart into separate selves again. Some of us ran out of breath before others. That's kind of what I listen for when I'm writing a line. I try to break it before the breath of it runs out or the energy of it gets too ragged or breaks, unless that's exactly what the line wants to do. Does that make sense? It's kind of a fractal to my approach to the poem, being alert to it, to how it wants to move, to how it is manifesting and then staying out of its way. But this is instinctive and so sounds a little strange when articulated, doesn't it? How the practice manifests the way forward each time and defies being cornered or bridled. So there's that.

THE BACKDROP OF CONSTANCY:

Karen Solie and Amanda Jernigan

Amanda Jernigan: I admit I've been feeling (excited, but) shy and formal about this conversation. After all, we've never met. We don't even know the same people, which is kind of amazing given the smallness of the Canadian poetry world. Well, I'm sure we know lots of the same people but it's remarkable the extent to which our circles haven't overlapped, actually. So I come to this with no preconceptions about who you are or what you're like beyond what I can glean from your work—and that's always a dangerous game. I read through your work, all the way from the beginning, and then your small chapbook *Retreats* arrived hot off the press from Junction Books and I read it and read it again. I'm enamoured of it: the scale of it, the structure of it, the individual poems and then the whole-greater-than-the-sum-of-its-partsness of it. So I've just done what I'd do if I were writing to a friend about his or her new book, which is to pour myself a generous glass and reread the book from first to last, and then sit down at my computer with the safety off my restraint just enough to try and say something about the poems (or rather, *ask* something about them).

There's a return to religious language in *Retreats.* I say "return" because I feel from the earlier books the backdrop of religion in small-town Saskatchewan. Religious language crops up in various poems—"Prayers for the Sick," "Lift Up Your Eyes," "I Let Love In"—usually in an ironized way though sometimes with a cast of longing. (I think too of that poem from *Pigeon* about myth and a Sunday school drawing, "Jesus Heals the Leopard.") But here I feel you're taking up religion and religious language in a different way: the irony is still there, and the longing, but it's a more sustained consideration, particularly around this practice of the retreat which of course is something that poets, as well as religious solitaries, engage in. The speakers in this book often have mixed feelings about retreating: they do it (and who *doesn't* want to retreat sometimes from this world) but always with a question about the ethics of it. Is it a failure of courage, a sign of defeat? Can it lead to enlightenment or does it lead precisely in the opposite direction? Can withdrawing from the world help us see reality more clearly, or do we see reality less clearly when we withdraw from the world? Which reality? Which world?

The book is framed and structured by the story of Ethernan. Is this based on a historical figure? Wikipedia gives me Saint Ethernan, who met a bad end on the Isle of May—is he your man? If so, how did you come upon him? How did you light on the idea of using this story to frame the sequence? And one other thing I'd like to ask, a bigger question: The poet Richard Outram wrote, "It may be that love and exile are the hope, perhaps the redemption, and modern condition of poets certainly; perhaps of all who care for language and the pursuit of understanding, possibly wisdom." Your work tends to be suspicious of anything that announces itself as hope—certainly of anything that announces itself as redemption—but do you think it's true that love and exile are somehow the condition of poets? Or the modern condition of poets? Or the proper condition of poets? Or the unfortunate *lot* of poets? Or are *all* creatures in exile? That's the freight of the quotation from Saint Augustine with which you begin (or Ethernan begins, or nearly begins) in *Retreats*.

Karen Solie: Thank you for so generously initiating this conversation. I too find it curious we've never met though undoubtedly we've been in the same room on occasion, haven't we? I'm not terribly gregarious and perhaps you're not either. As you say, it's dodgy to assume a writer's character on the basis of their work but maybe we've haunted our own corners of some event or other. I appreciate your attention to my poems, to their language. And yes, religious language, the scriptural, has always been present in my writing even when its syntax and diction aren't overtly so. Its cadences and tone are hardwired in me, I think. I was raised rural Catholic. When I was a child in my maternal grandparents' parish, masses were still sometimes read in Latin and the rituals of sacrament were dramatic and scary. The language of scripture and its music were complicated thrillingly by authors I read growing up—Shirley Jackson, William Faulkner, John Steinbeck, Flannery O'Connor, the Russian writers my dad loved—whom I found in the Bookmobile or on my parents' shelves. I recognized the echoes and progressions of this language in some of the music of my childhood too—in what's now called "classic country," in blues, folk, bluegrass and the beginnings of Americana or alt-country. I studied classical piano from early childhood through high school and heard it there too. Maybe it's just that I was registering pattern in a familiar way. Maybe this is all retroactive recognition, I don't know.

I hadn't thought about the poem about the Sunday school drawing, "Jesus Heals the Leopard," in the context of longing before, but I see it. In the early days of my religious education, it was all "Jesus Loves Me" and "God Is Love." In the poem, children in my sister's Sunday school class are asked to draw a picture from their favourite Bible story and the child, of course, has misheard or misremembered "Jesus Heals the Leper." The drawing is brilliant. I have a copy. It's funny and sweet but heartbreaking also in that before the stories of judgement, torture, despair, revenge, there are just wounded creatures being healed, and that dies hard in children.

At some point the fear and guilt Catholicism can inspire were supplemented for me by anger. These dark aspects existed simultaneously with a lingering attraction to the cadence and the beauty of the psalms, the desire for certainty even in the notable absence of it, the potential for humour, irony and longing realized in the writing and music I loved. My usage has hoped to gesture toward all of that. Again, this feels more intentional in hindsight than it perhaps was at the time. This language is simply part of the way I think. As is the language of work and of my family, who are very practical, curious and funny people. I'm no longer religious in any respect, but following a period of wholesale simplistic rejection I found writing that prompted me to consider its value toward a kind of secular spirituality whose practicality does not deny wonder and mystery, whose comforts lie alongside anger, fear and despair without seeking to resolve or deny them.

All of this, Amanda, wants to arrive at your question about exile, which is complicated. In his *Confessions*, Augustine writes that humans in this world—by virtue of original sin and insurmountable weakness—are exiled from God and from Paradise, but more interesting to me are his meditations on our exile from other creatures, other humans, from ourselves, from all we can't know. This non-knowledge is a God-shaped hole, but one that doesn't need to be filled in order to pursue the contemplation of mystery. Artists and philosophers, both religious and secular, have for centuries put uncertainty, the unsayable, the unknowable, at the heart of their work. "Bewilderment as a poetics and an ethics," as Fanny Howe says. And as you write in the *Days* section of *Years, Months, and Days*: "O wake / me from / the sleep / of being / sure."

So in Augustine's thought, all poets are in exile because all creatures are in exile. But then again, exile suggests a place we have known, where we have belonged and which we have been forced to leave. If one is religious, I suppose this idea rings true. Or, maybe it does if one believes we possess some kind of intuitive essential knowledge as children that we lose as we age, which I don't. Still, though, there is room in this metaphor.

I'm leery of the aestheticization or romanticization of exile for the obvious reason that there are people in literal exile for whom this condition is one of great peril, but also because it promotes an idea of the poet as someone who is apart, who is a special case, and I don't believe that either. This notion of the poet as estranged, as occupying by necessity a land apart, is antithetical to living in uncertainty. It curls up in a warm place of confidence in one's special status, even if it is felt as discomfort. It drains the spirit of Augustine's philosophy inside which I think one can adapt "God" and turns it into a popular narrative in which the poet—not of this world, misunderstood—becomes a romantic figure.

While Writer-in-Residence at the University of St Andrews in Scotland, walking for the first time along the Coastal Path between Anstruther and Crail, I came across the Caves of Caiplie. They're beautiful remnants of a cave system and in research I found that they've been sites of pilgrimage of one sort or another from antiquity. A seventh-century hermit called Ethernan purportedly withdrew from his conversion mission to spend an indeterminate period in the Caves while trying to decide whether to establish a priory on May Island—a small, intense, cliffy, optical illusion-inducing thing in the Firth of Forth directly opposite the Caves. It's not as weird as the Bass Rock, but close. Fabulous stories abound about Fife's early medieval monks and hermits but I could find little on Ethernan despite a cult having grown up around him, evidence of which still exists in place names and ancient inscriptions. He was said to have lived a long time as a hermit on bread and water—not that interesting. And many texts conflate his story with that of Saint Adrian, who was indeed murdered with his monks on May Island during the Viking raids of the ninth century.

Ethernan's retreat, as I imagine it, involved a pretty high degree of physical and psychological strain. He was faced every day with May Island, the embodiment of his choice, a choice basically between life as an "active"—a member of a community of scholarship and service—and life as a solitary "contemplative." Wars for wealth and territory among the tribes of Scotland and England raged during his time and the Catholic Church was realizing the power potential of its colonial project. Around the passages inspired by Ethernan—needless to say I am in no way attempting to write in the voice of a seventh-century religious hermit—are poems that orbit to varying degrees the Caves and Fife through the ages and that try to think about violence, wealth, power and religion; about belief, despair and responsibility. I hope also to address the complications of retreat. It can signify a period of concentration, work, solitude and self-denial. It can mean an abdication. It can mean self-protection, even cowardice. And in contemporary wellness culture it can mean self-indulgence. Sometimes we might not be sure into which we've retreated. I can't generalize about what writers do or should do when they retreat. I do think it's important to keep this question alive though for the writer and for the work. I imagine the Ethernan figure plagued by the question of whether his retreat is an act of courage or cowardice, haunted by the spectre of error and wrestling with indecision.

You write eloquently in your afterword to *Years, Months, and Days* of that book as a gesture extended from your secular context to the Old Order Mennonites whose texts inspired it as an attempt to ask "what can be carried across the boundary… between religions, or between religion and secularity." You also write of the poems as "meditations on the possibility of translation." What do you feel are the possibilities of translation, literally and figuratively, given that its possibilities are also, in some ways, its limitations? *Years, Months, and Days* also collaborates with a composer, as does your chapbook *The Temple*, another mode of translation.

Jernigan: Translation is one of those marvellous words that seem to mean all things. When we talk about translation in the context of language, we tend to emphasize translation as continuity, thus Samuel Johnson's definition "to change into another language retaining the sense." The emphasis is on what can be retained. But sometimes translation is used in almost the opposite sense, emphasizing discontinuity: translation as transformation. In *A Midsummer Night's Dream*, Peter Quince's astonished acknowledgement of Bottom's transformation from a weaver and amateur thespian into an ass is, "Bless thee,

Bottom, bless thee! Thou art translated!" That double sense, translation as continuity/translation as discontinuity, allows for some wonderfully ambiguous uses of the word, in both secular and sacred contexts. In *The Merry Wives of Windsor*, Falstaff purports to be able to "English" (translate into English) "the hardest voice of [the] behaviour" of a woman on whom he's set his sights, and his friend replies, "He hath studied her well, and translated her will, out of honesty into English." I think anyone who embarks on a work of linguistic translation—particularly when we're talking about poetry, which Frost once famously defined as "that which is lost in translation"—worries that in some sense she's translating her subject "out of honesty" (which in Shakespeare means, among other things, chastity) even as she translates it into English. There's a feeling of violation and this can be particularly acute when one is dealing with a sacred text. Tyndale, that early Englisher of the Bible, paid with his life. On the other hand, translation can be a form of devotion. It's a way of living closely with a text, of opening oneself to a text so that in the act of translating, one may find *oneself* translated, transformed by the words with which one is working.

In the English Bible, the word "translate" is used around the boundaries not between languages, but between doubt and faith, life and death: "By faith Enoch was translated that he should not see death…" or "the Father… Who hath delivered us from the power of darkness, and hath translated us into the kingdom of his dear Son…" These are startling transformations and the use of the word "translate" in these contexts makes me wonder about the continuities and discontinuities that are involved. Whatever one believes or does not believe about the kingdom of heaven, one can stand in awe before the ways in which we are translated in the course of our lives as human beings: translated out of nothingness into somethingness in our beginnings; translated from children into adults in the course of a life. I think of your poem "All That Is Certain Is Night Lasts Longer Than the Day": "Look at your past, how it's grown. / You've known it since it was yea high. Still you, / as you stand now, have never been there. Parts worn out, / renewed, replaced." And eventually we all get translated out of life into death, from somethingness into nothingness again, or from something into something-elseness, depending on your perspective.

When I call the small poems in *Years, Months, and Days* "meditations on the possibility of translation," I would hope to sound all these complicated senses of the word. I'm thinking about the possibility of the hymns being translated from one language into another, or from a particular tradition into a particular personhood, but I'm also thinking about the possibility of a particular person's being translated from doubt into faith (into doubt, into faith, into...), from life into death (into life, into death, into...), and through and across the years, months and days of a human lifetime. I'm thinking about both continuity and discontinuity. I didn't translate in its entirety any of the Mennonite hymns that were my source texts. I was working, rather, with those moments—often very fleeting—in the hymns that I felt I could understand, not just linguistically but "spiritually," if I can say that. Often these were moments of doubt and darkness; sometimes they were moments of longing. The sense of the passages is altered by the very act of excerption. By removing them from their contexts, I obscure to some extent the fact that in the hymns the moments of doubt or darkness are assimilated into a larger structure of faith and light.

Solie: Archetypal images of the grave, the harvest, new growth, are fundamental to the work in *Years, Months, and Days*. The poems are fragments, hymns, simultaneously precise and expansive. Their progression, in my reading, is from *Years'* melancholy attachments of grief—"before you were / I did not grieve you; / now you are not / I cannot leave you"— to *Months'* transformations, to a present tense in *Days* that is insistently awake and receptive, forward-looking. The *Hymns*, then, send this out as voice. Transformation seems to me to be both, to use Howe's phrase, "a poetics and an ethics" in this book and in your work as a whole. Does that feel accurate to you?

Jernigan: I ordered the poems in *Years, Months, and Days* intuitively, responding to their music as well as to their themes, but reading them now I can see that there is the sense of a journey here. Not necessarily specifically a journey from doubt to faith but certainly a pilgrimage of sorts. A work of travelling. And travelling is a form of translation, and translation a form of transformation, as I have said. I've always loved the classical stories of metamorphosis. After my first son was born, and partly to maintain my sanity amid the radical transformations of new parenthood, I began working on a series of poems that are meditations on those stories: short, ten-line poems in slant-rhymed couplets, the consistency of form serving as a foil for the metamorphic content, and giving me a shape that I could work with in my mind while I was nursing a baby or pushing a stroller or lying awake in a child's darkened room in the middle of the night.

But: transformation "as a poetics and an ethics." I'd like to think more about that. I do think my poems court "the beautiful changes" (the phrase is Richard Wilbur's) even as they acknowledge—as Wilbur's poem does—that that which is beautiful is subject to change. And they court the beautiful changes because, well, change is life. Death is a change but in another sense it is the end of change. I think of the psalmic image of Sheol, the pit, as a place of morbid stasis, a place cut off from the beautiful changes—the contingencies—of light and life.

Solie: Though you locate your upbringing in "the briar patch of secular skepticism," Biblical archetypes, along with those of myth, literature and history are touchstones in your work. We all have touchstones, ground we return to (as your section title in *Groundwork* identifies, "first principles"). What is the potential of return in a poet's work? When does it speak beyond familiarity? And how does return inflect and reflect transformation?

Jernigan: If the *Metamorphoses* is the great book of transformation in the Western tradition, then the *Odyssey* is the great book of return. I thought about the *Odyssey* a lot when I was writing *Groundwork*, and the final section of that book, "Journeywork", is all about the *Odyssey*, the twin labours of travelling and waiting that animate its principals, Odysseus and Penelope—who for me can be separate characters but also separate aspects of a single character. Near the end of the *Odyssey*, Odysseus and Penelope go off to bed together, returning to "their old ritual" in a bed that is literally rooted in the earth, having been carved by Odysseus from a standing olive tree and the chamber built around it: a beautiful image of permanence, of being able to go home. But this image is part of a story and the story tells us that it's also true, as in the Thomas Wolfe title, that you can't go home again. (I see we've circled back to the question of exile—speaking of return.) Odysseus's home has changed in his absence and he only manages to reassert himself there by means of terrible violence. And Odysseus himself has changed. The man whom Penelope confronts, sitting across from her in the firelight, is a stranger: "Sometimes she would look at him, with her eyes full upon him, and again would fail to know him…"

As a poet, I return again and again to these stories and I find that like Odysseus I both can and cannot go home to them. I go back to the *Odyssey* now (in Lattimore's translation, my favourite) and its words are exactly the same as I found them in my twenties. At the same time, I find that the story has changed or I have changed or both. I find this fascinating. I think the great stories are endless wells: we can draw from them again and again over the course of our lives because of their (and our) capacity for transformation.

Since I wrote to you initially, you've sent me the manuscript for your new book, *The Caiplie Caves*, which I love. All that is in *Retreats* is there, but now I can hear the fuller contexts you're sounding. I wonder if you might speak a bit about the role and/or the nature of the interlocutor(s) in this new book. It's a book about solitude but in which the question of address—the presence or absence of an addressee, the nature of the addressee(s)—is always present. Often the poems feel like letters or like dispatches from the field. A "you" is very movingly present at the end of "A Plenitude" ("the poppies you loved // parked like an ambulance by the barley field") and elsewhere, too: "I don't need to tell you what I thought" or "I can't have you back. My imagination's / not that good." There are also these moments where an other appears, if not as addressee ("I woke to a human noise originating outside me, for once"): the apparition of Paul, the woman who at one point provides the Ethernan figure with food and conversation. "A thought indulged in isolation is almost certainly an error:" that line crops up in one of the Ethernan poems and seems to express an important thought in the broader context of the book.

And another, perhaps related question: You spoke in your first response about the writers you grew up reading: Jackson, Faulkner, Steinbeck, O'Connor... Are there living masters (okay, problematic word, but anyway) who are important in your work? As influences or as interlocutors? *A thought indulged in isolation is almost certainly an error.* Does the thought of particular readers' eyes (and/or ears) on your work shape your work?

Solie: Thank you for your reading of the new work and for the notion of the poems as letters, dispatches. I think this is true even though I haven't thought about it in those terms. And like translation, maybe this could be said of all poems. There are times in the new book when its dispatches are addressed to people who will not receive them. "A Plenitude" is one of these, as is "The Meridian" from which you've also quoted.

A PLENITUDE
Karen Solie

Appearing as though they originate in spiritual rather
than material seed, as proof

we don't know how to properly celebrate
or mourn—bindweed and ox-eye daisy, cranesbill, harebell,

haresfoot clover, whose ideology is fragrant
and sticky, the underside of thinking blooming

across centuries. Arguments for and against belief
volunteering in equal profusion.

My many regrets have become the great passion of my life.
One may also grow fond of what there isn't

much of. Grass of Parnassus—
and when you finally find it, it's just okay.

But look for lies and you will see them everywhere,
like the melancholy thistle, erect spineless herb

of the sunflower family. That the eradication of desire
promotes peace and lengthens life

is not uncommon advice; still, you can't simply wait until
you feel like it. The beauty of the campions,

bladder and sea, the tough little sea rocket,
is their effort in spite of, I want to say, everything,

though they know nothing of what we mean
when we say everything, it is a sentiment referring only

to itself. Purple toadflax, common mouse ear,
orchids, trefoils, buttercup, self-heal,

the Adoxa moschatellina it's too late in the year for,
I can hardly stand to look at them.

And all identified after the fact
but for the banks of wild roses, the poppies you loved

parked like an ambulance by the barley field.

Other addressees are more general, or perhaps less defined, even to the speaker. In a few of what I've been calling "the Ethernan passages," the figure speaks to a hallucination or considers people from his past but in most his interlocutor is himself. Or it's whomever or whatever we address ourselves to when we think. It's the direction of our thoughts' gestures. "A thought indulged in isolation is almost certainly an error" is a fraught line for me and in some ways sits at the heart of the book. I have tried to release error as one of several ghosts into this manuscript. Aren't all thoughts indulged in isolation? Even if we consult others, incorporate ideas, synthesize them, revise accordingly in an unending (one hopes) process, when it comes down to it we are alone with our thoughts and with the ever-present spectre of error. The question is, given this, how to go on?

Howe says in a condition of bewilderment. Guided, says Wisława Szymborska, by the phrase, "I don't know." One poem I return to is an early one by Czesław Miłosz called "Encounter" which ends: "O my love, where are they, where are they going, / The flash of a hand, streak of movement, rustle of pebble. / I ask, not out of sorrow, but in wonder." Though "wonder" might feel impossibly generous at times, bountifully impossible, the poem is a question that does not stop being asked and its philosophy very difficult and beautiful.

I don't write to particular readers but maybe I'm fooling myself about this; maybe I don't intend to but do. I definitely write in the company of writers I read. They are many and various and include songwriters but in the writing of this new manuscript, a constellation formed. C.D. Wright was alive during much of the writing and if anyone will forever remain "a living master," she will. Fanny Howe has been another guiding light. Also Dionne Brand, Alice Oswald and Anne Carson. As I say, there are others, but these five writers have felt primary in this latest work.

Speaking of Wright, your observation about returning to find change in the old stories reminds me of her poetic imperative to avoid at all costs the "unfortunate predilection for nostalgia" that can afflict poetry of place. As she writes, a "special obligation is incurred by writing at the source: the author's longstanding presence, in the present. The citizenry of such a poetry, be it populous, must be given their share of the yield and their comeuppance. Oil tanks must displace stacks of corn shocks, mothers end up with far less than they wanted from their sons; a father will die with his jawbone frozen open, animals drag a trapped leg through the rose bed." How I love it when she starts to riff. The point is that the same goes for return to an idea, a story, a text, the implications of which vary according to the contexts of its apprehension. Return must not only acknowledge change but generate it in thinking, even subtly, in order that return not be merely a retreat into a nostalgic identification masquerading as authenticity. As if an inflexible opinion or stubborn interpretation reaffirms a self in danger of being lost. Susan Stewart writes in *On Longing* that metonymic displacement of a nostalgic sense of loss onto an object, a time, an idea, is to make of those things a kind of souvenir. "The double function of the souvenir," she writes, "is to authenticate a past or otherwise remote experience, and, at the same time, to discredit the present. The present is either too impersonal, too looming, or too alienating compared to the intimate and direct experience of contact which the souvenir has as its referent... The location of authenticity becomes whatever is distant to the present time and space."

The imperative to return with difference is leading me toward the element of repetition in your poems. I think of "Poem with the Gift of a Timepiece" from *All the Daylight Hours*: "Time keeps its watch upon your pulse; / your pulse may keep a watch on time, // so let this be upon your wrist: // hold up, against its perfect rhyme, / that which is slant, and off, and else." I have to say, you write terrific short poems. I'm very envious. I can't do them often or well. You've sent me new work too, the twelve-line poems that seem to have walked out of the Bay of Fundy and to which repetition of words, of phrasing, of syntax is crucial. Not surprisingly, when one thinks of the tides, but repetition feels important to your work more largely. It's interesting to me how form, metrical consistency, feels less like regularity or stability in your work than like trouble for those ideas. Or maybe the effect is more like a time-lapse of vegetation growing. The principles of pattern and variation are active in repetition that enacts change and I'm wondering about how repetition operates in your aesthetics, your philosophy, and as a felt element in the poems you write and read. Or, perhaps, how does form? Does it have something to do with, as you say above, "the consistency of form serving as a foil for the metamorphic content"?

Jernigan: Yes, totally. I'm interested in the fact that in order to perceive change, we need the backdrop of constancy. Here it is, June again, and I'm struck by how radically different my life is right now than it was last June—and I see that because it's June again. Repetition and variation. I find variation in repetition deeply beautiful: the imperfect pattern. That's life, that's organic structure. All those cobbles on a cobble beach and all of them different. Or line after line of blank verse, each of them a line of blank verse and yet each different from the last. Lattimore's translation of the *Odyssey* is in unrhymed hexameter lines—a similar principle: variation in repetition. Reading it, I feel like I am hearing waves break on the shore. Such a sound is not monotonous to me. The endless identical *beep beep beep* of a cell phone alarm is monotonous and frightening. The variation-in-repetition of the sea is, rather, fascinating. I think my favourite poem on the subject of repetition is Elizabeth Bishop's elegy for Robert Lowell, "North Haven":

> The Goldfinches are back, or others like them,
> and the White-throated Sparrow's five-note song,
> pleading and pleading, brings tears to the eyes.
> Nature repeats herself, or almost does:
> *repeat, repeat, repeat; revise, revise, revise.*

Bishop ends with an address to her dear friend who has died (speaking of absent interlocutors):

> You left North Haven, anchored in its rock,
> afloat in mystic blue… And now—you've left

113

for good. You can't derange, or re-arrange,
your poems again. (But the Sparrows can their song.)
The words won't change again. Sad friend, you cannot change.

Lowell qua Lowell has gone from the world of time and change: his words won't change again. But *we*, the living, change, and we can read his poems. There's a sort of trick here by which poetry keeps itself alive.

You speak about my proclivity for short poems (and let me say that I admire *your* ability with a long poem: I stand it awe before "Bitumen" for instance). I think that all poems, but maybe particularly short poems, solicit repetition. If they are any good, we read them again. And reading them again, we find them a little bit changed. New meanings emerge. Lately I've been experimenting with poems that literally loop, like this one from *the sign of jonas*, the Fundy series that you mentioned:

EXCERPT FROM *THE SIGN OF JONAS*
Amanda Jernigan

stones to mark
the places where
whom you seek
isn't there

chill foxfire
in the rot
underfoot
there is that

able to raise
light of these
sticks, children
of those

"Children of those / stones…" is a reference to a line from the Gospel of Matthew—the Gospels being another great structure of variation in repetition, or repetition in variation, or whatever it is. World without end.

I wonder if we can end by talking about the sea. There's a marvellous epigraph to *The Caiplie Caves*. From Horace's *Epistles*: "It is reason and wisdom which take away cares, not places affording wide views over the sea." I feel like you set that line up at the beginning of the manuscript as both motto and provocation. The book both affirms it and denies it—or at least complicates it. You're writing now, you've told me, from "a rented flat in a village on the Fife coast near the [Caiplie] Caves." I am about to move to a house by the sea. (Both of us, I note, were born inlanders.) Can I ask, what do you see right now when you look out your window?

Solie: It's unusual given that front matter is most often written last, but the fragment from the *Epistles* is where *The Caiplie Caves* began. It's one of the first notes I recorded when the book was yet a vague idea, when I was still writing poems toward *The Road In Is Not the Same Road Out*. Nearly seven years have passed and though I've enjoyed some wide views over the sea in that time, not too much of the other things I'm afraid.

I have two very different sightlines at present as the place is tiny. Over one shoulder is the A917, the Anstruther Road, which is what Crail's High Street becomes on its south end. Across the road are the gardens of, I've just realized, the Holy Trinity Catholic Church. Through the opposite window is a view of the Firth of Forth and May Island. The May is looking very dire and remote today though at other times it appears beautifully green, at peace, almost near enough to swim to.

THE STRIKING OF A BELL:

Russell Thornton and Phoebe Wang

Phoebe Wang: The first book I read of your work, *Birds, Metals, Stones & Rain*, felt like a culmination. What struck me most vividly about your poetry was its uncluttered diction, its plainsong. There's a notable quality of accessibility and earthiness, yet it's far from simple. This quality is something I strove—am still striving—to achieve in my own work. Was your sense of diction present in your earliest books or did you arrive at it later?

Russell Thornton: In the handful of years before *Birds, Metals, Stones & Rain* I was lost in income-getting. I was blackening pages but not typing up many poems. So if I reached a culmination with that book, I wasn't aware of it. Who knows what my unconscious was doing while I was occupied with bills and debts; time takes care of culminations whether you think you're involved or not. At some point, I read through my notebooks, concluded I had a manuscript and sent it off. It felt like the first time I'd done that sort of thing.

I can say that uncluttered diction and accessibility are important to me. I don't go to poetry to be shown how clever or fashionable or purposely befuddling a poet can be, or how self-admiringly quirky a poet's images or references are; I go to poetry to be ushered into the depths of human experience—ordinary or strange and dislocating or both—through language. I see genuine poetry as carrying out imaginative operations that have no truck with murky diction and inaccessibility.

Of course, accessibility is a tricky notion. I think my favourite poems by others are understandable enough on the regular comprehension level, even by people who don't read poetry. At the same time, there's a weighty momentum in these poems; they're informed by deep awareness of the human situation and by astonishing apprehension of ideas. I feel they look back at us from the far side of complexity. I think of William Blake's "The Tiger." I think of Elizabeth Bishop's best poems, which are for me almost painfully clear and accessible. My inner list goes on. What about Ezra Pound's "The River-Merchant's Wife: A Letter"? I think it's an example of marvellously fine accessibility. I think you play off this poem in an uncluttered and meaningful way in your own piece after Li Po, "The Child-Bride: A Letter." I used to wonder why poets such as Shakespeare and Dickinson and Yeats appealed to me more than most other poets. Was it a coincidence that their poems were accessible yet held the deepest store of meaning and magic? I realized that for me they touch at profound orders of consciousness precisely because they achieve what I'd call a near-miraculously uncluttered and extraordinarily subtle diction. "Tomorrow, and tomorrow, and tomorrow" and "Never, never, never, never, never" are among the greatest lines for me.

Plainsong and earthiness are beautiful words. And the songlike, ritualistic aspect of poetic language has drawn me in since I was a small child. That religious quality in intense use of language—as in a chant of supplication to or praise of unknown, invisible powers—is at the core of what I call poetry. That chant within plainsong arises not only out of flesh, but also out of earth. There's a hypnotic medieval English poem that states, "Earth out of earth is wondrously wrought." I love that line.

I connect uncluttered diction and accessibility with passionate poetic utterance—and integrity. I think I see integrity in authentic poets. Is it a refusal to surrender to BS? I wonder what you think.

Wang: Your views on this poetry and how it should resonate deeply across time and space contain many echoes for me, though I arrived at a similar stance by different paths.

I'm drawn to using a more accessible diction partly because of the English that I heard at home growing up. My parents aren't native English speakers but they picked up idioms from movies and songs: Bob Dylan and Joni Mitchell. They're also both visual artists who are susceptible to absorbing their environment. At the same time, they connected me with my heritage by speaking Cantonese at home. My parents are fond of proverbs that stress humility and the ironies of life. I never thought I could write for the whole of the human condition because my poems are inflected with my identity as female, Asian, able-bodied, cis-gendered and a first-world consumer. Like you, conceits and cleverness for their own sake are a turnoff, and I'm drawn to poetry that carries a weighty momentum, like the striking of a bell. That is how I try to determine this thing called "poetic integrity," by knocking on the sides of a poem and seeing whether the whole thing disassembles.

As a student, I searched for poetry containing that sonorous quality. I craved combinations of words that would unlock worlds and send me careening into another time. I found it in poets like Theodore Roethke, Wisława Szymborska, Seamus Heaney, Elizabeth Bishop, Gwendolyn MacEwan, Bronwen Wallace, Margaret Avison, P.K. Page, Anne Carson and Al Moritz, who was my mentor at the University of Toronto. These are poets who have the ability to be incantatory and, as you say, hypnotic. These days it's Carl Phillips and the new generation of poets of colour, but I'm always restlessly searching for poetry that taps into those silver veins of power.

Yes, there is so much song in "earth out of earth"—we have come crawling out of earth and are laid back into it. I'm not religious but the idea of the religious quality of language as a "chant of supplication to or praise of… invisible powers" appeals. I wonder how language, song, poetry might be an act of faith or a plea to an invisible force since that was its original purpose, whether it be proverb or hymn. It seems to me we're more in need of such acts than ever.

Is writing an act of faith for you and is being in nature a part of your search for earthiness and poetic integrity? What kinds of truth can we find in the natural world that we cannot in that world of the so-called civilized human, and how might we bring those truths and messages into our poetry?

Thornton: It's fascinating how people's early lives spin out into adult destinies. And interesting to me how you and I had different childhoods but still intersect in certain ways. I remember when I was six or seven seeing my father's Bob Dylan records lying around. And my father, like your parents are now, was a visual artist. But my parents split up when I was eight; I didn't see my father after that. They'd had to get married when my mother got pregnant with me at fifteen. I grew up with my mother and my three younger brothers on welfare. Interesting too, how you and I acquired BS detectors. For you, it was your Chinese background, your Cantonese-language household. My own identity became clear to me around grade four: my brothers and I were white trash. My predominant feeling in my community was fear: fear of being without food and shelter, fear of not being able to stay together as a family unit, fear of local predatory men who sexually assaulted my "welfare witch" mother, fear for my brothers' safety… I felt fear and anger. It gave me a particular outlook; it alerted me to irony. No matter how many grades my brothers and I skipped at school or how many athletic awards we won, we were not going to gain membership in what we saw as "the club." We were not going to enter a door to any home more than halfway up the North Vancouver hill. The much wealthier West Van? I wanted to dynamite it. But the bottom line, default setting for me about what was human was clicked on in grade nine when I read the phrase Shakespeare put in Lear's mouth and saw we were all versions of "a bare forked animal." And there's the adjective a few words away: "unaccommodated." This was and still is the norm for me.

I like your test for poetic integrity: "…knocking on the sides of a poem and seeing whether or not the whole thing disassembles." Yes, authenticity doesn't topple at a tap or two. And I like your list of poets who access "silver veins of power." These days, I often get my glimpses of that power in places I don't expect. I picked up a Robert Burns Collected recently and suddenly the poem "A Man's a Man For A' That" pierced me.

Yes, I'd say that for me poetry is an act of faith. I don't mean religious faith. I use the word *God* in my poems, but to signify the unknown, as with the *x* in mathematics. And I love the Bible as a sublime literary work. "The Song of Songs" is my favourite poem. But I'm not religious in any conventional way. And so by act of faith I mean an act of life-affirming imagination. My touchstones in this are William Blake and D.H. Lawrence. I think great poems, no matter how harrowing the nightmares they may tap into, in their revelling in language say a supreme *yes* to life.

I've always turned to the natural world to align myself with what I feel are un-outflankable realities. Maybe civilization itself is, as D.H. Lawrence said, a disease. And nature is imagination itself, as Blake said. I love Wordsworth's rhythms and imagery but I can't locate piety in nature. What I can see in nature is ruthless creativity.

I view nature not only as the planet and its forms and processes, but also what I'd call the "natural person." As I understand, language came out of the human organism in relationship with the natural environment; language can't be separated from nature. Of course, language helps produce self-consciousness and divides humans from the natural world, and so it can be said that language allows people to see nature as outside themselves. I'd say that language also licences people to devalue nature and commit crimes against it—not unlike the way words help people to see other human beings as objects and exclude, degrade and treat these "others" in heinous ways. Still, for me, truly imaginative linguistic acts can reorient humans to nature and their deepest selves. I agree with you when you say we're "in need of such acts."

I was interested to read something you wrote about *Admission Requirements*. You mentioned you "struck upon the tone" that you had been "striving for… a kind of irony without bitterness." I wonder if you'd like to share your thoughts on irony. And I wonder if you'd like to comment on what you say in "Application Form": "Don't limit yourself to the space provided."

Wang: I had difficulty with tone because I was too married to meaning, to representation, but what I really wanted to evoke was a sense of the complexity of layered history and irony, of coming across unlikely meanings in a garden or in a memory.

I intended to write nature poetry but the more time I spent in nature, the more I realized that these so-called natural spaces were managed spaces, i.e. parks, gardens, farmland around the Ottawa Valley, the Rideau canal, Hogsback Falls, Victoria Island and so on. There's one irony for you—finding that places we think of as natural are sodden with violence or human presence. I couldn't distance myself from how landscape had been written about. This discourse surrounding place and ways of imagining place seemed to steep into the place itself, making layers as dense as soil.

So while I deeply believe that language came out of the natural world, the concept of nature is one that is produced by culture and language. I'm suspicious, as you say, of the way that language is then used to imagine landscape and inscribe values onto it. Lately I've placed more faith in how the body responds and remembers place. To not claim a landscape but to have it claim you. That became the project of my book, to ask, "What do we need to be admitted here? What is required of us to live, to navigate this place?"

At a later stage I added poems such as "Regional Transit," "Self-Portrait as a Diasporic Subject," "Application Form" and poems about the city and migration. With these, I began with the plainest statement I could and then built it up by undermining or qualifying those statements. This was a way I could point out my uncertainty. The most overt example of this is that you would think that as a Canadian, and being born in Canada, I would feel at home here and be recognized as a Canadian; however, because of my heritage that's not always the case.

I use irony to create a range of tones such as a quiet reversal in which what the speaker describes or asks for is not what is really desired, which results in a sense of loss. What I really want to avoid is the ironic as mode, removed from emotion. In "Application Form" I was thinking through how socially coded instructions embedded within language can betray us, and what happens when we're given a set of instructions that are impossible to follow and only serve to categorize us in reductive ways. So often when we're required to identify ourselves, the complexity of ourselves and our experiences is blurred.

Do you go through a similar process in finding the right "tone" for each of your books, and do you attempt to vary the tonal range of your work both within a collection and also from book to book? Do you make conscious decisions such as deciding on the voice of a poem or a book? I notice that for you irony appears mostly when the speaker finds himself mistaken and/or learns something from a situation or experience. It's as though each poem is a kind of journey, beginning with certain assumptions and veering elsewhere.

Thornton: I'd say that in my collections I've tried to be honest; probably this more than anything else has affected my attitude toward my material and/or anyone listening. I'd like my language to meet my subject. This becomes an exploratory process for me, yes. This process is intimately bound up with what I call nature as opposed to any concept of nature, and with my body as opposed to any concept of the body. All I can do, I figure, is try to discover a meeting place for words and experience. Wherever I stand in this, I'm going to be limited, as you say, by instructions. Language is a set of instructions. But it's also its own tool for transcendence.

I always feel my personal history asks to be signed up beyond any individual or community identity. I learned at an early age that the idea of a "Canadian" was seamed with irony. For a portion of my early life, I lived across the street from the Mission reserve in North Vancouver. The word *Canadian* didn't tell me or anyone I knew who we were as people. Now, only poetry tells me who I am—and it tells me I am no one. I'd say a poem begins somewhere and takes me elsewhere; it takes me to *the* elsewhere.

I speak about tone in different ways than you; still, I feel we're referring to linked apprehensions. I think in both our poetic perspectives and procedures we're addressing what Keats called, in reference to negative capability, "uncertainties, doubts, mysteries." I'd add that the address seems to me to be part and parcel of individual experience and necessity.

Speaking of "Application Form," I wonder if you see it as a core poem in your collection. I also find "Sudden Departures," "Self-Portrait of a Diasporic Subject" and "Custom Design" to be key pieces; they present your themes. Among other things in these poems, I'm struck by the imaginative pitch you achieve with imagery of homes and houses. You talk about your parents: "They shifted homes like changing chords." I love that line. Then there's digging up "our secondhand push reel mower, rust-haltered / jars of tiger-eyed marbles I dropped / like anchors under the house…" I find myself returning often in my own poems to imagery of houses.

Wang: Those poems you mention were added late and I don't know if they are core poems but they fill gaps in and add more tonal range. I worked with Dionne Brand on the manuscript and she helped identify what was missing. It's fascinating how a keen editor can help shape a book. In my case, to see what grew from my early vision of a slim, quiet book of garden poems. I'm grateful someone gave me the permission to be passionate and urgent and intimate in those poems.

Admissions Requirements is inordinately preoccupied with place, belonging and home. It seems that for people like us—whose earliest experiences are seamed with pain or instability—the idea of home as a place of unbreacheable security is a mythical one. For my parents and grandparents, who were already removed from their places of birth and ancestral villages, the idea of home as a mythic place of origins is dangerous. I imagined home as a place where my family, our stories and our bodies would be recognized, but does such a place truly exist except as a projection?

I feel that sense of loss and haunting in your poems about houses and homes too, especially in a poem such as "The Eyes of Travel" from *House Built of Rain*. There's a feeling of houses as animate, where we can see ourselves and our abandoned desires. In poems such as "Possession" and "Another View," about the house my parents rented when we relocated to Vancouver, I wanted to explore those desires to have a tenancy. Houses are a kind of container, a skin that divides the private from the public self, the familiar and the unfamiliar. This has further implications about who we recognize as outsiders, as foreigners or as strangers. I borrow from Sara Ahmed's notion that the stranger is someone we already recognize and who is projected as presenting a potential disruption to the social order. I wanted to explore the figures of the outsider and insider in poems about Champlain, historical forts, brickworks, parks, power outages and the city. Whoever is truly at home is the one who is the host and the guide; roles which have responsibilities, as does the role of the guest. My poems attempt to be a different kind of guide.

POSSESSION
Phoebe Wang

Before we could see any progress,
my dad dislodged the blackberry vines,
I got the hooks from under my skin,
though the dark fruit was never within

reach again. My mother determined
what belonged and what didn't in the cold
drawers of the earth. We scratched
among its root cellar and jam-packed layers.

By spring the garden bequeathed us
with its prior arrangements. Roses gaped open
like the faces of coma patients,
tame and wordless. We couldn't spell out

the initials on the gate, or accuse whoever
splashed that aqua on the siding and trim.
The laundry line with its low-slung smile
wouldn't drop anything. When we prised

the glass from its blistered frame
it only denied, denied, denied.
But the loosened Formica was an account
of hard use and pots boiling over,

of hands whitened with flour, lard and labour
as if the shadow of the bread-box
and nickel canisters were still smeared
across the countertops by an oily sun.

It took two days to peel off the wall-to-wall,
blast out the sticky-spots with a thundering
industrial sand-drummer and the hired help
in harmony with it. Underneath were diamonds

of walnut inlay that hadn't felt the lash of light
in years. We smell blown candles in every room.
It's a kind of welcome, like a meal
slightly burnt. We sense we're not alone.

Your poem "A Stranger" and the travel poems in *The Hundred Lives* movingly address a stranger as the only person the speaker can offer his words to. There's a feeling that every stranger is, or could be, a lover. There are many collapsed dichotomies in this collection: the absent as present, dreaming while awake, the simplicity of ritual within sacred mysteries. *The Hundred Lives* contains many stories of connections between travellers. Is looking through others' eyes a way for you to engage with different kinds of experiences? In your writing there also seems to be a faith that putting experiences into words will be transformative or bring "wondrous news."

Thornton: What you say about the idea of home being mythical and dangerous is quite interesting to me. Likewise what you say about strangers. The houses I lived in as a child were literally dangerous for me. As much as I hated school regimens, classrooms were havens where I could escape physical abuse. I feel that in the end you focus on ideas of home in terms of social and political realities, whereas I focus more on the personal and metaphysical.

Yes, for me, a home of "unbreachable security" (a wonderful phrase) was always a fantasy. Later, I imagined a mythical home, but mythical in the sense of being deeply real, not a distraction or a projection. I see concrete situations as levels or aspects of invisible realities. I admit it. Home for me is a site of an ongoing enactment of identity.

Here is where the "stranger" you mention figures in, I suppose. In "A Stranger" in *The Hundred Lives*, the stranger isn't a social outsider but rather the unknowable arising within two people in a romantic relationship. I'm not intimating that any stranger is a potential lover but rather how, for me, to love a person is to meet a stranger. I might call that stranger *a god* or *God*. In "A Stranger" I'm talking about a person I loved who died. In another poem in the same book ("Oriste"), I intend a social ramification. Every "stranger who walks in" embodies the divine— again, a god or God, as in the myth of Hermes.

The "wondrous news" in my poem "The Blood-Red Egg" is meant as a comment on the mutual recognition that can occur between two people. What I try to convey is that when two people see each other as who they truly are, they become a platform, so to speak, for the creative processes of an unfathomable identity. Their "home" isn't an unachievable phantasm; it's a real, constant, transformative source where that identity announces itself and is the "news" they carry.

Having said all this, I feel I should also mention that often these days I'm compelled to talk about home and identity in other ways. In a poem in my new collection called "Open" I detail a memory of stealing dozens of cases of beer. I shared the last of my haul with two Squamish friends. Then in the pre-dawn we killed dozens of salmon heading up a river to spawn. We were all caught in systems of privilege.

OPEN
Russell Thornton

Everywhere: *Open, Open.* Stores, banks. Stores, banks.
Gas stations. *Open, Open Later, Open.*
For as long as I can remember, I have thought about stealing.

Once I scoped out and robbed the Number Five Orange.
The storage cellar had a steel hatch at ground level
with an easily removable commercial padlock.

I shimmied down through the small square opening
and with the City Police Station a block away,
in perfect calm I hoisted cases of beer to an accomplice.

In the weeks after, I got drunk many times for free.
My most professionally carried out act of crime gone unnoticed,
I could not help it, I gave in, I told people—

drinking at the St. Alice in North Van,
bragging about the great cache in my car,
I ended up on the Capilano reserve,

and I and two old school friends shared the last of the Labatt.
Out in the river in the dark, we gaffed coho,
laughing as we arrested pilgrim after silver pilgrim

beginning its ascent to the top of the canyon to spawn and die.
The tide was coming in, sea and river water
moving together, wrapping around me

where I stood in pants and shoes swaying, tottering. We gaffed.
We chucked salmon into the now empty trunk.
I would take it home and eat it. They would take it home

and eat it, or sell it. We gaffed. The oncoming wild eyes
of the fish staring straight into the first rays of the late summer sun.
The angled mouths of the fish, the blackness: *Open, Open.*

So, going on from ideas of home and identity, maybe we can talk about poetry as a kind of abode. How do you see the role of poetry in your life, your career as a Canadian poet?

Wang: In comparison to your long-branched poetic career, my own is nascent. I'm still feeling the shape of it. Poetry and writing is an abode, as you say, and it has sheltered my life and given me structure to approach the ineffable and irresolvable. So while the poet works continually toward an end result, the practice of poetry is just as necessary and sustaining. When I was younger I leaned on poetry as a ritual, a routine and a mode of reflection. It's still that, but also a lightning rod for questions about those social realities and identity positions that we take for granted because of, as we discussed before, the way they are framed through language. Just as the poem reaches a stage where there is a moment of clarity, it's gone again and we must begin the Sisyphean task once more.

Please do let me know how you've sustained a life in poetry. Have you ever felt a time when poetry could not offer you sustenance, or when you questioned it as a valid mode for responding to the world? What have been the greatest rewards for you in your career as a poet?

Thornton: I often wonder about poetry as a response to the world. But I'm stuck with poetry. I never stop being amazed by intense lyrical utterances; the verbal music, the concentration of meaning—it sustains me. What is my greatest reward to do with poetry? Perpetrating what I might be able to believe is a decent poem.

Wang: I wonder if poetry has the same role regardless of nationality and locality and cultural identity, or if there are specific roles for Canadian poetry? If so, there's no doubt that it's shifting. I read Canadian poetry when I was younger with a sense of outsider-ness, wanting to understand the concerns of this country but also to see how they were being challenged. Only those who truly belong have the right to criticize. Is it possible to revise our national image through literature? For instance, by valuing works by Indigenous authors, can Canadians revise and reshape their damaged relationships to Indigenous peoples and communities, and address the gross injustices committed against them?

To contribute to our national imagination through poetry, to bring a bird's-eye view to unique experiences and narratives while exposing the seams and underpinnings of language, is a great responsibility and privilege. It's one that still exacts a conformity with expectations around the English language and what makes for good literature, yet this apparent conformity or accessibility can be a useful tool as difficult truths are more palatable when wrought with lyrical lines, narrative structures and poetic devices.

I see this strategy at work in your narrative poems that present social realities such as "The St. Alice," "Nogales Prostitutes," "Aluminum Beds" and many others in your earlier collections, *The Hundred Lives, A Tunisian Notebook* and *The Human Shore*. It doesn't surprise me that you're writing new poems about the tension between class, status and identity as you do in the very moving poem, "Open." Those concerns seem to be threaded through your entire career.

Thornton: This is what I can say about revising Canada's national image through literature: It would be marvellous to see school curricula feature far more works by Indigenous people. I wouldn't dispense with the study of the spirit-filling great works of the world's literature; still, books such as *To Kill a Mockingbird*, as fine as they are, seem to me to be out of place as centrepieces in Canadian education.

On the personal front, I'm interested in learning about the poetic procedures in Squamish-language poetry and stories of the place where I was born and now live. Way back when, driving a taxi, I took several people to the ninetieth birthday celebration for Louis Miranda, who was an illustrious Squamish chief for around half a century. When he passed away, he was one of the very few fluent native speakers of the language, if I'm not mistaken. Fortunately, classes are now available in basic Squamish, and the language is being revived.

I'm grateful I've had the opportunity to learn a few Squamish words, among them the Squamish names for North Vancouver creeks and rivers. It's been exciting for me. What I've always called the Seymour River is called Chay-chil-whoak. What I've always called Lynn Creek, whose lacy, greenish waters I spent a significant portion of my early life in close proximity to, especially where it levels out as it meets the inlet, is called Kwa-hul-cha.

Wang: Particularly in your poems about travelling in Greece, how do you remain sensitive to the fact that these are other people's stories? Your narrative poems are deeply compassionate and non-judgmental—how do you achieve that tone and point of view? Has there ever been a time when you witnessed something that you did not feel you had the right to represent? Do you believe that it is possible for poets to simply tell a story, without inflecting it with their own bias?

Thornton: No, I don't think it's possible to tell a story or produce a poem without bias. I think human beings create their works accompanied by their biases, their limited perspectives. There are always going to be multiple perspectives. For me, this doesn't mean that the truth doesn't exist or can't be experienced; rather, it places on a writer the deep onus of imagination.

Wang: It is indeed an onus, and yet one that uplifts. Like being told you have all the expanse of sky to stretch out in as long as you can accept a single bird's eye view. Thank you, Russell, for your perspectives and words that show me what horizons are still ahead.

GETTING AWAY WITH SOMETHING EVERY DAY:

Tim Bowling and Raoul Fernandes

Tim Bowling: I've been wondering how we might start and after a while I decided that all my questions seemed superfluous. Weldon Kees, the American poet who killed himself in 1955, phoned his friend Pauline Kael just before he vanished (jumped off the Golden Gate Bridge) and asked her, "What are *you* going through?" That often strikes me as the only real question. But since we hardly know each other, I thought I'd edit the question: "Where are *you* at with your poetry these days?"

Raoul Fernandes: Wow, I love the urgency with which you framed that question. I wish I could say that what I'm going through and where I am with my poetry are closely related questions, but I'm in a period where my writing is taking a back seat to other things in my life: library tech school, working part-time and being a father to six-year-old and one-year-old boys. I've been taking little dips into writing now and then, but not a lot of sustained practice. I'd like to think I'm working on myself, my mind, whatever it is that writes the poems as I go about my day. Trying to keep the instrument tuned despite the perpetual fog from lack of sleep. I still feel the urge to write, and miss it, which is reassuring.

Bowling: I remember that fog quite well (three kids born four years apart) and am probably still in it, though the teenager-fog I'm in now is thicker, with a slightly different funk, of course. But the poems in *Transmitter and Receiver* read as if they're natural extensions of your day-to-day self, at least in their employment of the quotidian event (I'm thinking of the title poem, which arises out of a pizza delivery). So it's likely you're working hard on poems by simply living, which is a pretty darned good method. You're obviously the kind of poet who likes to get the whole world into your poetry. There's a powerful impression of a sensibility journeying through and participating in the familiar channels of life. Is that sensibility quite close to your actual nature?

Fernandes: I get a bit squirmy thinking about "my nature." I will say that I do hear from some people who know me that they see me in my poems. Or at least, it's not a total disconnection. I wonder if it's not so much about the subjects of the poems, but the way I move through the thoughts and images. That said, I feel there are some aspects to who I am that aren't quite present in the work. In person, I'm a bit sillier. I say foolish things more often. I've noticed moments in my writing where I might have presented myself as wiser than I am, forced a line that's very poetic, but not quite true to how I feel. I'd like to pay more attention to that. I want to be more honest in my work while staying weird and playful.

I'd like to put the question to you, you have such a strong grounded voice, even in your earlier work. I think of the ink of your poems as having a high percentage of your own blood. You seem to really care about getting it *right*, whether you're writing about childhood, or animals and nature or people you have known. Did you find that voice easily? Also, are there parts of you that don't go into the poems?

Bowling: I agree completely that there's something dangerously false in the poetic voice on the page. Or, rather, something limited about it that relates to a conscious performance. I mean, if I was as melancholy as I often appear in my poems, who could stand to be around me? I couldn't even stand to be around me. Yet I try very hard to avoid posturing and phoniness. As Auden said, "Nothing's original, only authentic." If I've been authentic in my poems, it is, as you suggest, a groundedness that comes from my sense of responsibility to a particular place and the people who inhabit it. And that place and those people—the south coast of British Columbia and its residents, including the animal residents—are under constant threat of vanishing, so I guess that explains the melancholy. But the blood! I have to laugh because your comment reminds me of this time I found my first book on a university shelf and some smart guy or gal had gone through it and circled the words *blood* and *bloody* wherever they appeared. It was a massacre! My only defence is that I grew up in a salmon fishing family, so I had plenty of exposure to blood, not to mention guts. Anyway, it turns out that you know the place of my poetry quite intimately, having spent some time in Ladner or Tsawwassen for part of your childhood. I gave a fist pump when your poem "Night School" started off with a reference to taking the 601 into Vancouver. Boy, I remember taking that bus. Took it regularly for almost thirty years. Used to take it into the city to borrow poetry books from the old main branch of the library on Robson Street. Also to meet up with the North Van poet Russell Thornton. I'm delighted that the 601 is a poetry bus for others too. Smarter people than me will say we're not supposed to respond so enthusiastically to the local in literature, but if that's so, I like not being so smart.

NIGHT SCHOOL
  Raoul Fernandes

We took the 601 into the city, double-clicking
catchphrases in raw throats, a beer bottle
rolling in pulses down the bus aisle. All the skulls
on all the hoodies in the Rock Shop
laughing at us on our arrival. Laughed back
from our own skulls. Being hustled
on the art gallery steps, smoking the oregano anyway,
smiles carved into our faces. Friends who appeared
like giants by our town's driftwood fires, now slapped
pale and diminished in this crowded light.

Asking for it, even. That monk's mud-puddle shove.
A night school that could teach me something about
night itself. It was slow education. My head
a Walkman that kept eating cassettes. For all I knew,
the glass office buildings were full of sorcerers
and dark arts. Missed the last bus home, wrote
a run-on sentence in my notebook, watched
it slink off the page and scribble darkly
through the streets. Years later,

I'd be living here, still editing that sentence, my old bicycle
winding past cherry trees towards the public library,
or for coffee with a friend. I'll cycle through
whole neighbourhoods I didn't know existed back then,
roads with islands of traffic-calming circular gardens, tulips
coming up bright and swordless in the spring air.

Can you talk a bit about your background on the coast, and how that experience works its way into your poems?

Fernandes: I moved to Tsawwassen with my family when I was fourteen on a cold New Year's Day. The only thing I remember from that evening is looking out the car window at the dark, snow-covered trees. It was a very different place from where I was coming from (Dubai), so it was pretty magical and also fit with my romantic idea of what Canada would look like. I only realized later that we happened to arrive in an unusually snowy winter.

So I spent my teens and early twenties there, and like many of the young people in small towns, I'd get itchy to bus into the city for more of a thrill. That's in part what "Night School" is about. A bit later, I also would take the 601 bus alone to go to the central library and read poetry, just like you. I miss that. But the town offered some wonder too—the dyke down near my house in Beach Grove was a frequent late-night hangout with friends—with a driftwood fire, out-of-tune guitars, experimentation of various sorts. I would also go down there by myself in the day just to walk around, look at the rocks, shells, herons, feel sad and lonely. I was *that* kind of poet. But I did feel distance from nature even though I loved being in it. The noise in my head and the noise of the world could not be quieted enough to really feel a part of nature.

Reading your poems I see a more visceral connection to the land and water. You are right there in the mess of fish guts. And there are meditative moments like communing with an owl in "Snowy Owl After Midnight": "each hunting in his way / the small gifts of the night" or a dying salmon in "The Last Sockeye." It seems you pay attention to these animals as a way of unlocking and entering your memories and inner life. And yet the creature is still very *there* with its "rotted eyes and scales like bloodied coins." I think you really get that balance right. I've always felt that the minds of animals are one of our deep mysteries. It seems that we try really hard to connect but we can't help seeing mostly ourselves.

Bowling: Animals? Raoul, you really don't want to get me started on this subject. I'll just say that as I've grown older I've developed a greater appreciation for other species. And I suspect that you're right: our relationship to animals is almost always a form of self-exploration. Do you know there are now more pets than children here in Edmonton? And I'll bet that statistic is true in many other places. Yet our whole way of life is violently anti-animal. So much so that when I see a wild creature—a coyote, a porcupine—I either feel like crying or apologizing, despite the fact that they have absolutely no concern for my emotional or psychological state. Anyway, Tsawwassen in the snow is indeed magical. Good timing on your arrival! But it must have been weird to live there, especially coming from Dubai. I remember reading that Tsawwassen was once voted the whitest town in Canada. Down on the mud flats, we always referred to Tsawwassen as Snob Hill (even though I had, and still have, family living there). I think Tom Selleck of *Magnum, P.I.* fame once owned a fancy place up on the Bluff.

Fernandes: Whoa, I didn't know that about Selleck. That would have impressed fourteen-year-old me. But yeah, it was super white. Still is, but I think it's changed a bit. I was one of two or three brown kids in high school when I got there. I think I sort of expected it, not realizing at first how multicultural the rest of BC was. I think having girls in the classroom was more overwhelming for me as I was coming from a Catholic school where boys and girls were separated.

I never heard "Snob Hill." Ha, there's definitely some truth to that. I remember Tsawwassen kids turning their nose up at Ladner but I couldn't see it as anything but childish posturing. Maybe the smell from the fields, too? Anyway, I didn't quite fit in until I found the weird kids, the goths and punks. They were sweet and kind of accepted me for the awkward kid that I was. There's something about the squareness of the town that makes anyone strange and creative seem like a really precious thing. It's such a contrast. You can see how that fed into some of my poems.

I still didn't know many poets back then though. I actually knew more writers through the Internet. What was it like when you were starting out?

You mentioned Russell Thornton—a wonderful human being. I can see a lot of connection between your work and his. I also meet a lot of young writers now who, through school or university, have started their practice with other writers around them. I can't imagine it.

Bowling: It's a completely different world now. I didn't know any other writers until I was in my late twenties, and I certainly never took any creative writing classes (didn't even know they existed, in fact). What was it like for me? Lonely. Very lonely. I wouldn't wish that loneliness on anyone. But it helped me develop as a poet, that's for sure. Robert Bly once said that the problem with creative writing programs is that you're always supported, that you're never allowed to fail. I can't speak to the truth of that, but in my pre-Internet apprentice days, I sent out submissions in the post, received rejections in the post and tested myself against the poets I admired. Failure? All the time. But the tide finally turned as it tends to do for a fisherman. Your comment about walking alone on the beach really resonates with me because I spent a lot of time walking by myself down the long farm roads of west Ladner trying to figure out how to make a life in poetry. Somehow or other I've managed to do so, but there was never any useful map for the journey. Still isn't one, as far as I know.

Fernandes: It's probably good that there are different routes to take. Mine was a bit odd. I took a couple creative writing classes in college, right after high school, with the fine poet Patrick Friesen. I cringe thinking about the poems I wrote then but somehow he saw something in them and encouraged me along. That was a big deal to me. I ended up dropping out of college but kept writing, reading more widely and filling up notebooks with bad poems over the next several years. I also had an online community through livejournal, an early blogging platform, and shared my poems there. I took excursions into other arts: painting, music, photography (great for loner walks!) but poetry was always at the centre. At some point I decided to take it more seriously, so I did The Writers Studio at SFU which gave me the last kick I needed to start putting a book together. It also introduced me to the writing community in Vancouver.

I have mixed feelings about the workshop environment. It can be good. For me, it wasn't about getting particular poems fixed up, but learning how to think through what's going on in a poem. Being a bit more conscious of them and what one is doing in a broader context. If a workshop is good, you're still allowed to fail, I think. The poems, and your ego, can take quite a beating. What's troubling is the pressure to make your work conform to what people consider a good poem, which can scrub out interesting idiosyncrasies or bold risks. I think it's good at a particular stage for some writers, but I don't feel much interest in it anymore. I have a few trusted writer friends that I run my poems by once I've done all I can with them.

I think I read that you're teaching now? Do you run workshops at all? I can imagine you telling students to put down their smartphones, go walk into the wilderness and not come back until they have one genuine thought. Ha. I'm only half kidding.

Bowling: I've done a little teaching over the past few years, but I'm down to a course a term at most, and likely will soon stop completely. Like Delmore Schwartz, I'm a grotesque before the classroom, a vaudeville clown. He used to get so anxious about lecturing that he'd just read out loud for the whole class (and apparently he was a mumbler). I can relate. In fact, if you read my latest novel, *The Heavy Bear*, you'll see that it's all about a sessional instructor named Tim Bowling who becomes so haunted by the bear-shaped ghosts of Buster Keaton and Delmore Schwartz that he can't face going to his first day of classes. But in real life, I like the students and admire anyone who tries to be creative. I just always feel like I want to protect writers and writing from the institution. And since I'm a writer, I want to protect myself, so that will inevitably mean that I'll go back to the knife's edge of freelance writing that I've lived on most of my adult life. No guaranteed income, but no more mumbling, grotesque lecturing either.

Your joke about walking into the wilderness isn't off the mark. I'm currently writing a non-fiction book about modern-day hermitage, about withdrawing from the world. I'm no seer or philosopher, but I do hate those goddamned phones. Whenever one of my kids is staring at one, I just want to grab it and throw it on the floor and stomp it into a billion pieces. My eldest finds it hilarious that I still pay for everything with cash. But my job now, in many ways, is to be a source of amusement to my kids. It's work I'm happy to do.

Fernandes: Ha, that's my job too. I know what you mean about the phones. My kids are too young to use them but I have to discipline myself to keep from checking mine all the time. These devices, like a lot of things on the Internet, are designed to capitalize on one's attention. I feel that poetry matters in this context—so much of it is about what you pay attention to, both inside yourself and in the outside world. I sometimes wonder if it can be a way to strengthen yourself against these powerful distractions, to restore some control. Reading or listening to poetry requires an immense amount of openness and engagement. I think it's a struggle even for people who love it. I'm still amazed and heartened to see anyone at poetry readings, that people have chosen to come and listen to someone read poems instead of just staying in and watching Netflix.

Bowling: Digital devices. Like I always say, I'm not a Luddite, but I read their pamphlets. Seriously, my loathing for cell phones, laptops and social media makes me feel very cut off from my culture. Poetry absolutely depends on memory; there can be no use of language without memory. So these technologies, which basically erode our capacity to remember, are counter-productive for poets. Ah yes, but they're fun! Well, I play a lot of soccer. Imagine if someone said, "Hey, there's this new training program. It's great. Lots of fun; you'll love it. But over time using it, you'll lose the ability to run, to dribble, to pass and to head the ball." That's how I see digital technologies in relation to poetry. They're not going to help anyone produce memorable language but the cultural pressure to participate, to be contemporary, to stay in touch with the times is so great on us that we all succumb to it. How can we not? I don't have a cell phone, but my kids all do, and they use their phones to communicate. So, I'm going to have to get one of the damned things eventually just so I can get texts from my children when they're no longer living with me. Anyway, I'm proud to be old-fashioned, fashioned from the old (like everyone else). I'll keep writing my poems by hand and reading poems in physical books rather than online. And likely become more and more isolated. So be it.

Fernandes: I'd like to touch on your hermit leanings and how being in a "community" of writers fits into it. In 2002 you were the editor of *Where the Words Come From*, the collection of interviews which inspired this book. Through it, you fostered connections between writers of varied voices, poetic disciplines and at different stages of their careers. What did that project mean to you then and what does it means to you now?

Bowling: I want to be honest, but I also want to be fair to myself. On the one hand, I don't believe I'm in some kind of cultural boat pulling on behalf of a team. I've always resisted joining or participating in group literary activities; in fact, I think I became a writer primarily because I felt a need to be completely independent. On the other hand, I know first-hand the immense value of mentorship, of organizations that support literary production, of residencies that put established writers into contact with apprentice writers. I also know how critically important it is to have at least one fellow poet with whom you feel a powerful sense of kinship. So I guess I've always been conflicted about the whole idea of a literary community. But back in 2002 when *Where the Words Come From* came out I was thirty-eight with two toddlers and a newborn—in general, I felt more connected to the human community, including the community of poets, than I do now. At fifty-four, I find myself grateful for the opportunities that I have as a writer in Canada but my relationship to the culture at large has greatly diminished. My ambition is entirely for the work, whereas twenty years ago, I had more worldly ambitions and expectations.

Where are you at with regards to all this? You mentioned having a few important first readers of your poems and of course your first collection, by any account, was extremely well received. You also mentioned being a little apprehensive about putting the next collection into the world. So I'm curious to hear your views on the public side of the poet's life.

Fernandes: I've gone through some shifts with this. As I've said, my start as a poet was fairly solitary with only a vague community of writers on the Internet, which is its own kind of lonely isolation. After the Writer's Studio, I began to meet and connect with more poets in Vancouver and go to readings. I have to admit I found it thrilling. I'm no extrovert by any means, but I do like genuinely connecting with people, especially ones who are as geeky and passionate about writing as I am. Going for a coffee or beer with a fellow poet is still one of my favourite things to do, though I don't have many chances to do that these days. I'm still somewhat glad that a lot of my early development as a poet was outside a literary social sphere, though. Maybe it allows more friendships with the books on the shelf. But who knows? These days, more of my experience of the writing community is through social media. Through that lens, what we're calling "CanLit" is quite fractious and volatile, to put it mildly. I am proud and supportive of some of my writer friends who are doing more work for justice and change. But more and more I find myself wanting to retreat into a WiFi-less cabin with a pile of good books. I have to tell myself that my main job here is to sit quietly and write poems.

With the awards, I feel grateful, but cautiously so. When I got the nomination for the Bronwen Wallace Award, it gave me a boost of confidence and pushed me to start working on the book. And after publishing, the recognition has felt pretty great. I have to perform a bit of a mental trick to not let it feed the ego, though. Being on the other side of judging committees now, I realize how arbitrary the choices can be, at least in the final stages. What it boils down to is that some select people really like the book. But, you know, sometimes I'll get a sweet message from someone saying they read my poems out loud with their partner at their breakfast table. That feels more real and manageable than wearing a suit to a gala or having a gold sticker on my cover. Don't get me wrong, I was on a cloud when I got the news about the Dorothy Livesay nomination, but then the next day, sitting down to write, I was back in the muck and the should-it-be-this-word-or-that-word business. There's no room for any concerns about success or awards in that headspace, thank goodness. I think I'll have to manage expectations, both of myself and others, when considering the next book—but when I'm actually writing I don't want to be anywhere but inside the poems.

Bowling: Ah, the writing! That's what it all boils down to in the end. I've been sick recently with a nasty cold, and as I'm lying there in the middle of the night feeling all man-cold sorry for myself, I start thinking about life in that "real dark night of the soul" sense and the images and lines start coming. Before I know it, I've forgotten all about being sick. Poetry is health and sanity as well as joy and freedom. I don't know why or how I wound up being a poet but what a stroke of great good fortune. Being a poet, I feel like I'm getting away with something every day. After all, most people don't get to write poems, one of the most affirmative human acts I can think of. We're lucky, even without awards (but as you say, awards are most welcome. Who doesn't need encouragement, not to mention cash?).

That's nice about people reading your poems aloud across the breakfast table. Somehow I don't think mine would go quite so well that early in the day! But I know what you mean about that intimate connection. When I published my first book and launched it at my little hometown library, a whole bunch of people came out to support me basically because they knew my parents. Well, one of these people was the barber who'd cut my hair as a kid. I saw him a year or so later and he said, "You know, I don't ever read poetry but your book really made me look more closely at this place we live in." That was really meaningful to me.

So, where the writing's concerned, how do you know when you're ready to write a poem? Is there a feeling you get, like Frost's lump in the throat? Do you start with an image, a situation, a rhythm?

Fernandes: Most often I just decide that I'm going to sit down and write with no thoughts about what's going to happen. I like the show-up-and-do-the-work attitude rather than waiting for inspiration or the muse or whatever. I'd like to believe I can do it in different situations and headspaces, but I've learned that there are some states of mind that are especially difficult. I don't really want to write when I'm frustrated or angry. I like being calm and quiet. And when things are moving, it's like, yeah, a rhythm or a kind of hum. I usually start with an image or a thought that's been bouncing around in my head and see if it will go anywhere. Most of the time it doesn't and I have a pile of interesting phrases and images, but not a poem. Nothing to hold it together. That's usually my problem. I think there's a kind of poem that poets write that allows that kind of collage, but I can't justify it for myself. And when it does come together it seems to happen in a mysterious way that's hard to replicate.

How do you work out your poems? I can tell in some poems there's a central image, say in "Early Autumn: A Still Life" which begins with the image of a dead pheasant and a fallen apple on a porch step. Then you dive into the childhood memory triggered by that particular image. In other poems it feels like there is a kind of stance or even a character, as in the Tenderman poems, that is at the heart of the poem. I think what I'm saying is that I appreciate how grounded I feel in your poems and wonder how you do it. I also wonder if it comes out of the narrative skills you have as a novelist.

Bowling: I like that you use the word "mystery" when describing the process. I mean, ultimately, it is always at least partially a mystery how poems get made. But for me, especially early on, it was always about imagery and metaphor. In fact, I still believe that metaphorical skill is what really makes a poet. That and the capacity to sing. So when I find a memorable image, and then the right rhythm for it, I'm usually on my way. But patience is key, of course. I might wait months or years for the right marriage of image and rhythm. With the Tenderman poems, however, those definitely start with more of an attitude, a way of articulating many ideas and emotions about contemporary life, so even though they come at their own sweet pace (I'm currently working on another manuscript of them), there is perhaps some reliance on the novelist's sense of character and setting that brings them into being. I suppose I've always felt that all poems are narrative, in the sense that the poet is trying to communicate his or her experience of being in the world.

WHO WOULD STEAL A BIRD'S NEST?
Tim Bowling

Who would steal a bird's nest, tenderman?
In the full freshet flush of spring?
Yes, of course, *you* would,
But what you wouldn't steal
hasn't been made, or dreamed.
I'm talking about the ordinary desperate grasping human
who might steal and pawn his mother's
wedding ring—from his mother's *first* marriage,
I mean. The nest was perfectly constructed
and positioned, tenderman, like a military
drone between Cassiopeia
and Afghanistan, like a medieval
chastity belt. And the blue eggs
might have been gazing skyward
like the eyes of your own son
if you had one, and the mother,
like all mothers,
returned to the absence
of what she's loved so fiercely
(her wings broken as she flies).

Look at it. In the crook
of a dead branch. Wound
twigs in the exact
circumference of the crown
of thorns Christ wore,
only heavier,
though could anything be heavier
to bear than the sins of…

never mind, tenderman—
someone tiptoed up in the dead
of night and trembling possibly with love
took the question mark down from the question.

Fernandes: Yes, I like that. Poetry really is a lovely way to communicate the experience of being alive. I've also been thinking about how poetry has a different relationship with the movement of time than prose. Poems quite often stay within a single moment or only a few minutes transpire from beginning to end. It feels like that's one of the special things a poem can do. If it's not telling a story it can talk about something in a more vertical way.

There's a really great voice in those Tenderman poems. I've been admiring how poets use attitude and stance. It's addictive sometimes. As much as I'm fairly comfortable with my voice, I can't help reading someone great and thinking "I want to write like this!" Then I'll read someone very different and think the same thought again. I guess it's the way influence works, but I didn't expect to still have that reaction this far into the game. I'm curious about who you read when you were starting out, how they did (or didn't) shape your voice. And do you feel there is still some shaping going on with the writers you read now?

Bowling: Wanting to write like others seems perfectly healthy to me. I remember reading something this poet—it might have been Vernon Watkins— said on the subject: for every poet there comes that sad moment when he realizes that all the styles in the anthologies can't be his! I certainly remember wishing that I could write like Dylan Thomas but also like William Stafford. The great thing, of course, is that excellent poetry comes in so many styles and we have different voices inside of us that can come out to adjust our style as we go along. Early on I was enamoured of the big American modernists, mostly Williams and Stevens, and that led me straight into the next generation of Americans, Jarrell and Lowell and Bishop and Schwartz and Berryman, which led me into the next generation of Kinnell, Levine, Rich, Plath. The linguistic energy of these poets and their sense of the occasion of a poem as essentially dramatic had a big influence on me. Now? Over the past few years, I've read a lot of R.S. Thomas, George Mackay Brown, Tomas Tranströmer and Yehuda Amichai. And I keep going back to Adrienne Rich, whose work seems more important and powerful to me all the time. But I can't say just how they've influenced me except to confirm my love of metaphor, drama and integrity. I'll let you in on a dirty secret, one that I've heard other older poets whisper about: one can lose the desire to read poems even as the desire to write them remains. I mostly read non-fiction these days though it is sometimes non-fiction about poetry. I can't imagine not reading poems at all, of course, but I just don't devour them the way I used to.

Fernandes: I can't imagine stopping, either. Though I have noticed that I'm not as blown away as I used to be by poems—I admire them and am moved, but the experience is not "as if the top of my head were taken off" as Dickinson would have it. Not often enough, anyway. But I think I need to clear space in my head and heart to be more receptive to that.

I had a bit of a weird path with my reading. I still am embarrassed that I don't go far back into the past, other than when I was really into haiku and the old Japanese masters. Early on, I read the Beats, the New York School. I went through a Bukowski phase, a Richard Brautigan phase. C.K. Williams. Gerald Stern. Alden Nowlan. I love Levine, who you mentioned. I was obsessed with this young Arkansas writer, Frank Stanford, for a while—really dark, vivid stuff. I think you'd like him if you don't already know him. You'll notice that these are all dudes, and I've felt bad that my shelf was so lopsided in that way, so I've been consciously trying to remedy that over the years, mostly with contemporary writers. Recent favourites are Mary Ruefle, Dorothea Lasky, Karen Solie. All very different. I'm in a book club and we read Danez Smith's *Don't Call Us Dead* recently, which is very powerful (and probably clocks more use of the word *blood* than you!). There are dozens of local poets around me of course that I try to keep up with. Looking forward, I want to put a conscious effort into reading more poets in other parts of the world as well as further back in time.

One wouldn't draw clear lines between my work and the writers I mention here, but I think you get that there's something deeper than style or voice that comes through. Sometimes when I see a poet doing something new and unusual in a poem, I don't necessarily want to copy that same move, but it gives me more freedom or permission to do something weird and particular to me. That's a real gift.

Bowling: "Weird and particular to me." I like that. In fact, it might be as useful a definition of poetry as any. And maybe a definition of poetry is a good place to end our conversation. I get the feeling that we could go on for many more pages, but as the old chestnut has it, "less is more." Except when more is more and more is less and less is less. But these are rabbit holes for another day.

Take care, Raoul. Much power to your poetry!

Fernandes: Thanks, Tim. It's been great to go down these rabbit holes with you. Hopefully our paths will cross in the near future. All the best, and don't become a hermit!

CROSSING THE DIVIDE:

Elizabeth Bachinsky and Kayla Czaga

Elizabeth Bachinsky: I'm sitting here in a little park just off Granville Street and there's an ambulance helicopter going by and I've just spent the past hour and a half trying to find a spot in Vancouver on a sunny Sunday that isn't super loud and teeming with people, but I've finally found it. I'm so happy to be here to ask Kayla Czaga some questions. What can I tell you about Kayla? I know that she is a wonderful poet. I've known her for about six years. The first time I met her in person, she was my student at UBC in a publishing class I taught briefly. I was aware of her poetry because I'd seen it in journals around the country and I'd even juried a competition or two and selected her writing for prizes. The thing that draws me to her poetry is how smart and lateral her thinking is and how her voice is so likeable and unusual. Hopefully we'll get a chance to talk about that in a little bit. But first, I'd like to find out about Kayla and where she's coming from as a person. I personally find that stuff interesting, and I find her life particularly fascinating. Hopefully our readers will, too. Kayla, can you tell me a little bit about where you're coming from? I'm especially interested in the access to books and films and media that you had growing up.

Kayla Czaga: Okay, wow. I'm hoping that this will come back toward you a little bit, as we have to do both parts for this interview. I was born in Alberta, but I spent most of my childhood and youth growing up in Kitimat, BC, a place I left when I was seventeen when I moved to Victoria and then to Vancouver, around the time you met me. Growing up, there were some books in the house. My dad had a large occult book collection. Sometime in the seventies or eighties he got a catalog and paid like thirty bucks a month to receive these cult books in the mail, books about witchcraft and all sorts of wild things. He also had all these western romance novels. My mom was a big reader, a big fan of fantasy, sci-fi, and the YA spectrum. They read to me a lot when I was a kid. My mom liked to say that I could read *The Cat in the Hat* when I was two, but I could just parrot it back to her. I was a very bookish kid, but I wasn't very discerning. I would just read whatever was around. My dad would go down to the thrift store and buy armloads of whatever books and I would just read those and that was what my early literary education was. We watched a lot of action movies. I still don't like rom-coms because it isn't a genre I grew up with. I watched a lot of *Star Trek, Star Wars, Die Hard,* serious action movies. When I was sixteen, my dad decided I was finally old enough to watch *Pulp Fiction* with him. So my friend and I awkwardly watched *Pulp Fiction* with him. That's what I had access to growing up: a very small library. I just kind of read what I could.

Bachinksy: Right on! I love it when you talk about your dad. Do you feel willing to talk a little bit about him?

Czaga: Yeah, why not. He's my biggest role model/inspiration. Still.

Bachinksy: You had an unusual relationship with him, didn't you? Like he was a very progressive, awesome person, and you've said that you were raised to be a slut. What does that mean to you?

Czaga: ...my dad was a slut. He self-described that way. He was a bit of an objectifying person, but he was also pretty equal-opportunity in that he talked about going to rallies for women's right to choose to have abortions and wear pants and do whatever they wanted. He thought that women could be any-thing and respected his mom, who was this short, self-motivated Hungarian woman who raised three boys alone and ran a farm—so strong. And defin-itely as I was growing up, he told me he would know when it was time to take me to the doctor when he saw boys hanging around the house. Because he didn't think I shouldn't have sex or be pure in that way. He just wanted me to be smart and be curious and interested in the world. He took me fishing and taught me math. He was once laid off from one of his jobs and he just took a year to hang out with me and spend time with me and it was wonderful.

Bachinksy: That's awesome. I love it.

Czaga: Yeah, and he never once called me *pretty*. He called me *smart*. He called me *stubborn* a lot, which—what did you expect?

Bachinksy: Right on. I love that you said that he taught you math and that you are still into math. Tell me a little bit about your love of mathematics.

Czaga: I loved math a lot growing up; it was something I was good at. When I was sixteen, my dad and I had a bit of a feud because he thought I should go be a doctor or something and, I don't know, it felt stifling. I had to do all these hard courses and I was also artistic, so I stopped taking math. But, I've gotten back to it recently, especially since he passed away. He was so financial and so into number-crunching; it was something he was always doing, putting receipts on the fridge to keep track of. He thought of and processed the world in numbers. So, I've become kind of a junior accountant at work—I do the cash outs, I find the money. I'm looking into upgrading my math. Also, we teach math like it's in a little vacuum. Lately I've been looking into the history of mathematics from the Greeks, which was the study of knowledge, not originally just the study of numbers. The ancients had a more holistic view of what learning was and didn't have it as separated, so getting back to it at that level has been helpful to me: to reconnect with it and to also reconnect with my dad posthumously.

Bachinksy: So, you say you are kind of a "junior accountant" at your job. You have kind of an unusual job. Can you tell me a little bit about that?

Czaga: It's actually been the best job I've ever had. I work in a nerd bar, which is a bar that plays no sports but plays old sci-fi on the TV. It's called The Storm Crow. You can roll a twenty-sided die to get a randomized shot and a randomized burger. They're going to do a chain thing now, but it was a real Vancouver original. Sean Cranbury, a local man of letters (if you can call him that), got kind of annoyed with me always complaining about my dumb Starbucks job on Facebook. He was running this bar and was like, "Come and work with me." I had no serving experience and no idea what to do. I just showed up and started badly carrying drinks to people. I got a bit better. I wrote the bar's in-house dinosaur erotica and learned how to bartend a little bit. They were looking for somebody to help out in management as their overhead grew so I said, "You can train me to count your money." It's fun. Like doing a crossword except you get paid.

Bachinksy: Have you thought about pursuing a CGA?

Czaga: I have. We talked a little bit earlier, when we were trying to find a parking spot, about how I'm picky when it comes to finding jobs, and often uncertain because it's difficult to find a job you can build a writing life around because so much of our lives is touring and being in our own minds, and I feel like I have to devote so much time to that, that I'm like, "Can I be an accountant? Do I have time to do all of that and have the writing career I want?"

Because you've written five books and have a wonderful job, family life, child, I would love to hear a little bit about how you have managed to fit the writing life around your other life.

Bachinksy: Oh, wow, way to turn it around.

Czaga: I know.

Bachinksy: [*Laughs uproariously*]. Well, it has been challenging. When I first started writing, I was in my early twenties and had a lot of energy. I was keen and curious—I don't know where I got all the energy from. I was driven. I wrote all the time and volunteered for all kinds of organizations and studied writing at colleges and universities and just got involved wherever I went, or at least I tried to. And then, once I'd worked my way through school, I continued to work in the book industry; I was a bookseller for a while at the UBC bookstore at Robson Square and then started getting some contract work at universities teaching creative writing and that was pretty lucky. My first break was at Vancouver Film School. I taught one of Jen Currin's multi-genre classes, so I was teaching international students how to write screenplays and poems and that sort of thing. That was a good place to cut my teeth. Then I started working at a bunch of different places as well and built my CV that way. I never found it difficult to write when I was just working or teaching because I felt connected to my community and the practice of writing was such an important part of my life. But that changed a lot when I had a baby. It's been hard to keep the writing up through that. My job has also changed recently; I've become the chair of the Douglas College creative writing department and the work is much more demanding. I teach full-time and do administrative work and have a toddler and a marriage and all that stuff. So, for writing, it's been pretty tough. But, I mean, I wrote this morning.

Czaga: Awesome. I want to get back to your having a child and current situation, but I want to back it up and…

Bachinksy: Do you want to tell people about how you know me before you do that?

Czaga: Oh, yes. Elizabeth is just wonderful. I guess we were paired up for this interview because we match and I'm glad I get to talk to her rather than… I know this is supposed to be an older person/younger person interview, but I feel like I gel with Elizabeth on an interpersonal level. But then she is also so warm and open and thoughtful in a way that, when I was growing up, when I thought about what writers looked like, serious writers, I didn't picture Elizabeth. So her life gives me hope. I first read Elizabeth's work when I was in the undergrad program at the University of Victoria. Tim Lilburn loved *The God of Missed Connections,* Elizabeth's third book, and he described her as the next big thing in CanLit. Her work is amazing, and that summer I spent devouring *Home of Sudden Service* and *The God of Missed Connections* and…

I'm going to get back to the question now. One of the things that struck me about your writing is how peopled your books are, and how invested in family and friendship your work is. Can you talk a little bit about the role of friendship in your writing?

Bachinksy: Wow, that is super timely. One of the things I've been thinking about lately is how hard it is for me to maintain friendships and relationships with friends over time. Friendship is important to me. I moved out of my parent's house when I was fifteen and didn't work on connecting with my biological family until well into my adulthood. I love my family and we get along well now that I'm an adult but, yeah, it was difficult. So, early on in my life, I started to connect intensely with friends. I think I was looking for a family elsewhere. People talk about "chosen family" and I think I am a person who tried to find a chosen family. So, I guess maybe that would account for my trying to have deep relationships with friends. Of course now I have my own family, so things have changed.

Czaga: Have some of these deep relationships factored into your process as a writer?

Bachinksy: I would say yes because so much of my experience as a writer has involved travelling around the country and meeting people and getting to know Canada through the eyes of other writers. So when I go to St. John's, Newfoundland, I get to visit Mary Dalton and Don McKay and Russell Wangersky and George Murray and Elisabeth de Mariaffi. I get to see Gros Morne National Park through Sarah Tilley's eyes and those rainbow-coloured row houses through Beth Follett and Stan Dragland's. I consider that to be a real gift. I've been lucky that way, and it's been the same every place I've gone. There are always other writers waiting to meet me and take me around and show me things. It's been important.

Czaga: Do you want to tell our potential readers a unique story of you and another writer somewhere in Canada?

Bachinksy: Sure. The first poet who comes to mind is Sue Sinclair. I run into her everywhere! Montreal, Toronto, St. John's, Vancouver. Our trip to the Muskwa-Kechika was pretty amazing. Donna Kane, who's a poet living in Fort St. John, BC—her partner is environmentalist and photographer Wayne Saw-chuck. They lead these artist tours through the Muskwa-Kechika, a wilderness area and the largest untouched boreal forest in North America. Wayne and Donna do this so these artists will together generate a body of work and raise public awareness about the place. The Muskwa-Kechika is remote and endan-gered; the only other place you can see a boreal forest like this is in Russia. So I flew to Fort St. John in a Fokker, went to Donna's ranch, got in her little car with her and Sue, drove ten hours north up the Alaska highway, got on a little float plane at Muncho Lake, flew in the little float plane for an hour up to Mayfield Lake—which is right near the Yukon–BC border. That's the area of Canada we're talking about. And there was Sue.

Czaga: What did you see?

Bachinksy: The continental divide. Mountains, tundra—well not tundra, it's more like scrub, pine, quite a lot of rock, big mountains and valleys and lakes, but rugged. Not like cottage country in Ontario. It's the North. When you get to Muncho, it's a glacial lake so it's that emerald-green colour, almost like milky green. It's unbelievably beautiful. So, we're in this little red float plane and we get to Mayfield Lake and there's moose belly-deep in the water eating absinthe-green lakeweed and it's like, "Where am I?" And there're animals everywhere, bears and... Which isn't actually a completely unknown experience for me because my dad's a helicopter pilot so I grew up flying around the Yukon when I was young... Anyway, Sue Sinclair was there.

Czaga: Who's from the east coast.

Bachinksy: Newfoundland. Yes. Sue Sinclair was there. Sue stands out for me because she's a great poet and she was working on her Ph.D. in philosophy at the time. She literally wrote part of her dissertation in a tent on the shoulder of a mountain at fifty-seven thousand feet. It is about beauty and the sublime, which is apt because she's quite beautiful and sublime: a dancer, graceful, brilliant, all these things. I remember hiking with her. It was quite a trek, her up ahead with those antelope-like legs going up a 40 percent grade and me chugging up behind her. That was a singular experience. And then there we were in the forest riding the pack horses up to the base camp and she had this crappy digital camera with batteries in it but not the cap to the compartment, so there were these naked batteries sticking out the back of her camera and one of the batteries fell out while I was taking a picture of her—this is not the story she wants me to tell—into the mud and gone, because the mud was up to the horse's knees. And I was like, that's it, we've ruined the Muskwa-Kechika by dropping a battery in the mud. No one had been on that trail for, like, seven hundred years.

Czaga: That's a great story.

Bachinksy: Friends.

Czaga: Friends. In *Hottest Summer in Recorded History* almost every poem is dedicated to another person, most of them writers. How did that come about? Was it intentional when you set out?

Bachinksy: No, but when I was compiling the book I noticed that all the poems were written in different parts of Canada and for me it was like, *whoa*, I went to Winnipeg and saw Jon Paul Fiorentino at a festival and then I had this weird dream about handcuffs, or I was in St. John's and Daniel Deveroux ran into me on the road and I was like, "I'm going to get my nails done, where should I go?" So, it just seemed natural to dedicate those poems to those people because they shared those experiences with me and were a part of it. And, of course, I was reading so many Canadian poets then.

Czaga: That book definitely feels like a big conversation with a lot of voices.

Bachinksy: Yeah, and all the poems definitely have different lives as time goes on and people come and go from your life. Our lives change.

Czaga: When I first started as a writer I felt like everyone you met around the country was safe… You know, everyone was thoughtful and then—it wasn't until I read that wonderful Emma Healey essay, "Stories Like Passwords," and the UBC Accountable stuff started happening—you realize there're these shadowy people that you don't actually know in your community. It was a big turning point for me. And so your book is very different to read now. Has the shift in perception in our community affected you?

Bachinksy: Yeah. It's fucked up. Last night I was up until four in the morning reading about Junot Díaz and Sherman Alexie and all the shit they've been up to. It's awful. You know, the week I gave birth to Lydia was the week that the allegations about Jian Ghomeshi came out. He'd just put out his creepy letter saying that he was taking responsibility for things and we would get past this. It had that air of "this will pass." Do you remember what he said?

Czaga: He said something about how "I'm just into this BDSM stuff and people misunderstand me and I'm sorry if people felt hurt by actions"—a very non-apology.

Bachinksy: Yeah, so there was Jian Ghomeshi and others, and then there was another one… Well, they all just started to go down like dominoes. I've been saying to my husband that if I like a man's writing, it probably means they're a sexual predator. I mean, I'm standing in front of my bookshelf now and going, "Oh. God. Who else am I going to have to take off my syllabus?"

Czaga: Who was that guy who supported Steve?

Bachinksy: Oh, yes. Steven Galloway. There was Steven Galloway.

Czaga: There was Joseph Boyden. Fake-Native Joseph Boyden.

Bachinksy: Jian Ghomeshi, Joseph Boyden, Stephen Galloway, David Mc-Gimpsey.

Czaga: David McGimspey—that was hard to take.

Bachinksy: Yes. Very. And then nothing, just radio silence. Here's the thing: I knew that Jian Ghomeshi was choking women years before the allegations because I knew women who worked at the CBC who had said this about him and we still all listened to Q in the morning. I was always in the car commuting somewhere. I loved groaning at Ghomeshi's stupid monologues and then you hear this stuff and you're like, "What the fuck?" And sure enough the truth comes out. This was all obviously a long time coming.

Czaga: I feel naive but I was unconnected and quite young when all this stuff started happening, and it seemed to come from nowhere.

Bachinksy: Maybe we could turn the table a little bit and ask you about your experience as a student going through university, having the experience of this coming out.

Czaga: Well, I am extremely lucky to have had wonderful mentors, most of whom were female, but some who weren't. I worked with Tim Lilburn, Lorna Cozier, Steve Price and Carla Funk at the University of Victoria. Wonderful mentors who were not creepy with their students. I lived in a bubble and thought CanLit was wonderful and supportive—maybe a little bit mean sometimes because they were hard-nosed about good poetry—and then I came to UBC for my MFA and worked with Rhea Tregebov, who is the most

"CanPo mom" in existence. I worked with you, and Sheryda Warrener was my second reader. I was having a pretty good time out here on the west coast. Our matriarchs are Jen Currin and Amber Dawn and you. I thought I was in a paradise. Something you were saying about being a member of a community and volunteering, and when I was coming up it felt so worth it to go to all the events, to volunteer all your time because CanLit was this thing that I believed in. Then, the chair of my department, the year after I graduated, was fired for breach of trust and very serious allegations. I've kind of been saying "fuck it" to a lot of things since then. I know it's important to volunteer and go to all these things, but it's also okay to say...

Bachinksy: *No.*

Czaga: No to things.

Bachinksy: I agree.

Czaga: It feels a bit selfish, but I didn't realize what was going on for a long time.

Bachinksy: Now that we do realize what is going on, how's that changing how you read or write?

Czaga: Well, I didn't read male prose writers for two years. It was a conscious thing. All the CWILA counts were coming out about how often women's books were reviewed. And then I just recently saw a thing about how women's books are priced at 45 percent less than men's books, on the whole. I've definitely changed; I don't just read what the chair of the department wants me to read. I definitely think we need to support other voices and voices that are not getting the broadcasting they deserve because they don't belong to this men's club or because they don't have a buddy in CanLit.
What about you? How do you feel?

Bachinksy: I feel like since the whole Ghomeshi, Galloway, Jeramy Dodds mix—now joined by so many cultural icons—have been outed for creepiness, for sexual assault, that has put a temporary kibosh on my writing, that in combination with a toddler at home, that was really a double-whammy that made me stop and assess. I've been reading *The New York Times* like crazy—we haven't even talked about the larger political moment we're in that is so strange and not so unfamiliar to Canadians who lived under Steven Harper for a decade. It's a very strange moment we're in. But I feel like now, with the #MeToo stuff that has been coming out in the last seven months, I feel a real momentum that gives me a lot of hope and permission. So I'm feeling more hopeful. Last night reading about Díaz I thought, *Wow, this is really going to change.* They aren't even giving a Nobel Prize this year. Did you hear about this?

Czaga: No!

Bachinksy: Yeah, the Nobel Prize for Literature has been cancelled because an academy member's husband had eighteen allegations against him for sexual assault. So, no Nobel Prize for Literature this year and they'll give two next year. We're talking about major shifts going on in the cultural moment.

Czaga: Also, did you hear that Kendrick Lamar won a Pulitzer? Which was the first non-jazz album. Off topic completely but it does feel like there is a convergence. Like the institutional background is shifting away from a ...

Bachinksy: A white male paradigm.

Czaga: Yeah; it's interesting.

Bachinksy: It feels pretty awesome that things are changing, and obviously "God abhors a void," so who is going to rush in to fill the void when these major male players are gone? It's women of every lived experience and orientation. LGBTQ writers. We're going to start hearing a lot more stories from writers whose writing has been pushed to the margins and those stories are going to become mainstream. I have to believe this because the thought gives me hope. If you think about your life, you're a queer woman living in Vancouver and your lived experience is fully, 100 percent, mainstream to Kayla Czaga. Do you know what I mean?

Czaga: Sorta ...

Bachinksy: I mean your lived experience is your mainstream. Why shouldn't your stories be brought to a larger readership? They are stories that move people. My experience of living is not marginal. It is common.

Czaga: I do see a shift in what stories are being told, read and winning awards, but it is hard to be as hopeful as you are. If there's a change of tide one way, there can also be one back the other way. Like, if we look at American politics, which is super disheartening, we can see how extreme those tides can be.

Bachinksy: It's fucked up.

Czaga: Yeah.

Bachinksy: Now I'm thinking of He Who Shall Not be Named. Some of the hateful stuff he has spewed. But I'm even grateful for that because that type of misogyny...

Czaga: The rise of neo-fascism?

Bachinksy: ...it is refreshing to hear the POTUS speak these misogynies so publicly because you can't pretend it's not there. The danger is in plain sight, unlike with people like Díaz or Ghomeshi who hide behind progressive rhetoric. Misogyny gives me a clear path, a real motivation, a constant reminder that writing is a serious matter. I take that freedom seriously. It's such a privilege to be able to do it. But, also, it's fucking fun. Writing is fun.

Czaga: Yeah!

Bachinksy: Or it can be.

Czaga: I love it; it's my favourite thing.

Bachinksy: Tell me about that—why do you love writing?

Czaga: I don't know. I mean, yes it is fun, but it's never a thing I have to think about doing; it was just a thing I did when I was a kid. I think about it more now because we overthought it in university and I'm like, "Do we have to approach these things in these ways?" It's just my response to the world. Singular.

I would love to hear more about your *play* because you're a very formal and procedural person, and you have a lot of tricks—not tricks, but...

Bachinksy: Methods?

Czaga: Yes, and you have a lot of play in the forms, which is not a thing I'm particularly invested in.

Bachinksy: I would have to disagree—you are invested in forms, but not in the way you're thinking.

Czaga: But you approach things in a different way.

Bachinksy: Let's think about it like this: I want to talk about that poem you have called "A Girl Like You." So, the formal constraint that you are using in that poem is repetition. You are coming back to the refrain over and over throughout the poem, which has a way of tethering you, keeping you in one place. You can go off, but you always have that strong spine that brings you back to what is going on in that poem. So that's a formal methodology: a method that brings you back to what is important in the poem. That's true for me too. When I'm working with a particular subject, I feel like it's pretty important to find a method that is going to suit that subject. There's always a kind of methodology at play that gives me focus.

Czaga: I did not intend that poem to have a refrain. It didn't come out of that; I kind of put it on later, then took it off in some spots and messed around with it.

It seems that some of your work begins with a methodology, but I usually begin with a line and then the methodology might come in later. But it seems like you are more connected to the original process.

Bachinksy: I guess it depends. I do generally work in modes: content before form/form before content. Of course, in the best of all possible worlds, form and content are working together harmoniously, because I believe in both. Some of my books were written one way and some were written another. Right now, I'm just collecting stuff and waiting to see what comes of it. Last night, I wrote a thing called "Literal Things that Literary Men have Literally Said to Me" and it's just a list of little quotes, you know? You don't know who said them, or in what context, but it felt so good to write it.

Czaga: Maybe that's the poem we can put in the book.

Bachinksy: Yeah, sure. [*Laughs*]

LITERAL THINGS LITERARY MEN HAVE LITERALLY SAID TO ME
Elizabeth Bachinsky

Don't Worry. I'm a chubby chaser.

You remind me of my wife.

She's not my wife.

You have a very symmetrical face.

You're like my sister. My sister I'd like to fuck.

Are you ovulating right now?

Women have it so much easier in publishing.

I only have one testicle. You wait. You'll see.

Keep writing.

Czaga: I love that idea. You also talked about how sometimes it's one way and sometimes it's the other way, and I'm like, "I've done that in the past." You've written five books! You have an impressive collection of spines on my bookshelf. You've got a lot of words behind you.

Bachinksy: Wow! I look at them and think, *That's not very much.* They're such slim volumes.

Czaga: Which is good, right? It means you know how to edit. But five books— that's a great career so far. When did *Curio* come out? 2008?

Bachinksy: 2005.

Czaga: Right, so you've been publishing for thirteen years. How has your writing and publishing changed in that time?

Bachinksy: I've been so lucky; I've had good publishers. Book*hug is my first press; they published my first book and my fourth book. My fourth book, *I Don't Feel So Good*, was a fundraiser for the Chris Reimer Foundation so it was more of a favour from the press than a solicited book. I called Jay up and said, "Jay, what do you think? I would love to do this project," and he was like, "You bet." I'm so lucky that I have those kinds of great relationships. And, Nightwood Editions—I'm so happy with them. They have published three of my books, my more mainstream books, the narrative stuff. Silas is a right-on fella; he does a lot of good work on the Sunshine Coast and in the writing community.

Czaga: He is great. I was glad my first book had a home there, too. But the process of writing itself—I know you aren't right now feeling connected to it, but the poems you were writing for *The Hottest Summer in Recorded History*, how were they different from the poems you were writing for *Home of Sudden Service*? Or was it the same, has it always been consistent?

Bachinksy: In *The Hottest Summer in Recorded History* there are poems where I was just living my life and being a writer—you were talking about wanting this desire, too, to live your life and be a writer—and the world can just leave you alone. That's a powerful desire. Of course, we should just live our lives and process things around us. That seems to be a pretty productive way of being.

All those poems in *Hottest Summer*, I wrote them out when I was travelling. The only difference between *Home of Sudden Service* and *Hottest Summer* is lived experience. I wrote *Home of Sudden Service* in my early and mid-twenties. Linda Svendsen, one of my mentors, once said we always write about things that happened ten years ago. I wrote some of the poems in *Home of Sudden Service* when I was twenty-two years old. So, it's a book about my youth, a kid in the Fraser Valley getting up to no good. If you look at your first book too, you'll see that. There's your family and all these stories about young people and their Epi pens. It's true. And your next book, which I totally want to hear about...

Czaga: I forgot about that. I have a book coming out.

Bachinksy: Those poems were written in the past decade, too.

Czaga: That's true, although I did go back to youth quite a bit, at least in the first major section.

Bachinksy: How could you not?

Czaga: My first collection came out so quickly, and then I was like, "Oh, all these things I didn't write about."

Bachinksy: So, tell me about your new book. It's coming out with House of Anansi in 2019. What's it called?

Czaga: *Dunk Tank*. I'm so glad that everyone—well, I'm sure *someone* will have a negative reaction to that title, but I've had like eight different working titles, and that's the one that people have been like, "*Dunk Tank*. Good Words. Yes." So, I feel pretty strong about it, and the poem "Dunk Tank" works pretty well as a title poem. It's not the crazy-good, best poem in the book, but it has all the themes. So, I got my contract and got my edits and then my father died unexpectedly, so as much as my next book is on my radar it is also not on my radar. I'm just thankful that I wrote so much that I can just... It's really hard to edit stuff that happened before a major life event.

Bachinksy: Yes.

Czaga: I had a long manuscript and I got some great edits, substantive edits, from my fantastic editor Kevin Connolly for some poems and I was like, "I'm just going to cut this poem." I like short books. I like your spines. It's weird that the book feels so super old to me and it's not even out.

Bachinksy: Well, I'm very excited about it. The poems in the book aren't old for me. And they are so lively and punchy. I was so lucky to have you visit my classroom a month ago. My students loved, you by the way.

Czaga: I loved your students. One of them came into my bar. Santiago Ureña.

Bachinksy: Santiago is amazing. I bet they'll have a book. Brandi Bird, too. Carleigh Baker is wonderful, too.

Czaga: I taught one of your students, whose work I loved as well. She wrote these wonderful, slight poems in long sequences. She worked in the library. I did one-on-one via email with her.

Bachinksy: I do love my students, and they did love you. And we especially loved your Winona Ryder poem where her pores are like eyes, and if it seems like she is looking at you, she is.

Czaga: "Death Starring Winona Ryder."

DEATH STARRING WINONA RYDER
Kayla Czaga

Her eyes are the three faces of Cerberus.
The third hides behind her shocked bangs.
No, the third is her pursed mouth. If you zoom
in on Winona you will see her skin
is filled with third eyes—we call them pores.
Each one of them is rolling. Each one
of them a head to the dog guarding Death.

Of course an actor covered in third eyes
that also guard Death would be difficult
to work with. What did you expect?
She has the most magical acne. You may feel
her whole body making eye contact with you
because it is, but mostly her whole body
has better things to look at like very
long trains and sexy rivers. If the dogs
guard Death then inside of her is where
all the dead people live. All the living people
live outside of her eating pretzels etc. like
you and me. Wow, she is extremely
haunted. Ever thought Beetlejuice felt
a bit too same same to your home
movies? Me too. All our Ouija boards call
out Winona during sex over and over.
It would be boring if it wasn't Winona.
Don't call her a bitch though she is covered
in bitches and sometimes they are in heat.
Sometimes you can smell her skin—it smells
like it just ran into the yard and murdered
something so quickly you didn't hear it
die, but when Winona dies what happens?
What will happen to us when Winona dies?

Bachinksy: It actually reminds me of the same vibe as—you know, our favourite.

Czaga: Matthew Zapruder?

Bachinksy: Hmm… no… Ugh, that's what happens when you turn forty-two. You lose words… Mary Ruefle!

Czaga: That makes me so happy.

Bachinksy: You know, a little off-kilter, unexpected.

Czaga: I didn't know that I have an off-kilter, lateral way of thinking. My editor talked about that too. I was like, "I see things differently? What are you talking about?"

Bachinksy: I love that about you. It's fun to come along on that ride with you as a reader. Your poetry is a real glimpse into how you see things.

Czaga: I love how that connects to what you were saying about living your life and how you process it in these ways. It's a real personal/public way to process things.

Bachinksy: Absolutely.

Czaga: And then it goes on to have a life that other people think about. Do you have a good story of a poem taking on a life outside of you?

Bachinksy: You're so funny, look at you! You're like, "Come on, Liz! Have poems taken on lives without you?" Totally, they have. There are poems out there that I look at and think, *Good work little poem*!

Czaga: Our transitions in this conversation are on point. Talk about poems that have taken on lives.

Bachinksy: Obviously, the one that is totally outside my control is "Wolf Lake."

Czaga: Oh, the Matt Rader poem.

Bachinksy: Yes, the poem inspired by Matt Rader's "Wolf Lake." They've told me that, for a few years, it was one of the most popular poems for Poetry in Voice, Canada's national recitation program for youth. Something like thirty thousand English or creative writing students participate in Poetry in Voice every year.

Czaga: It's a major honour, I've heard from other poets, to have your poem recited by so many youth.

Bachinksy: You're going to have this experience at some point; it is truly a chilling experience. You're like, "What is happening here?" So, "Wolf Lake" won that competition a couple of years in a row, and—

Czaga: Matt Rader's version or yours?

Bachinksy: Mine. Yeah. It's just a total trip to see those kids on stage reading it and overacting it. It's crazy. And you know, Michael V. Smith made a film of my version and of Matt's version and might make a film of his own version. There are three versions of that poem, so it's like a multi-voiced experience. And since it's a little film, it's been shown all over the place: New York, Beirut, Australia. It's weird to see a poem get legs. And even Margaret Atwood—and I know we don't love Margaret Atwood anymore—but she was like, "That was a good poem." And I was like, "Margaret Atwood just told me I wrote a good poem."

Czaga: That story touches all of the things you've talked about today: process, taking a different person's poem, community and then this greater thing that is happening outside of us.

Bachinksy: Do you have a poem that has taken off without you?

Czaga: I love talking to people about what they're reading. I read all the time, I read on the toilet, I share, I do it privately. So being read, having someone else approach me and read me without me knowing about it feels so intense. One of your students said that they included my Livejournal.com poem—which is about a sad northern youth connecting with online communities and self-harm and stuff—in a collection of poems for their partner and read it to them. That was a super intimate experience that made me feel so many different things at once. I love that.

Bachinksy: It is a trip to think that this thing that you've done privately then crosses the divide and lights up someone else's imagination. It is amazing, truly amazing.

Czaga: I feel like that is the perfect endnote.

NINE-TENTHS UNSEEN, AN AFTERWORD:

Sue Sinclair and Nick Thran

Nick Thran: So we've got this peculiar invitation to co-write an afterword for a book of conversations between Canadian poets, the follow-up to *Where the Words Come From: Canadian Poets in Conversation*. We both remember from that volume a question Ken Babstock asked Don McKay in their interview "The Appropriate Gesture, or, Regular Dumbass Guy Looks at Bird," back in 2002:

> **KB:** "Your partner, Jan Zwicky, is also a poet and a professor of philosophy, what would we overhear at the breakfast table? You losing?"
>
> **DM:** "How about another bagel?"

Babstock moved off quickly, perhaps sensing an invasion of privacy has occurred, calling his question "stupid." Yet I suspect McKay just wanted to make sure Babstock understood that the purchasing, toasting, buttering and digesting of bagels is at the fore of the daily life of two people living together, whether they both happen to write poems or not. McKay might have gone at least *a bit* further, if given the chance.

We've now read all of the interviews for this new volume. We've been told we can dialogue, that we can duel it out, write in separate echo chambers or experiment, collage. You and I exert a lot of effort trying to balance our creative, bill-paying, and domestic lives together. We also exert a lot of effort trying to create pockets where each of us can be in our *own* heads and think about our *own* projects, often at the expense of time for conversation with each other about poetry and poems. What Rob Taylor has offered us here is an opportunity to converse in a way that is actually quite rare for us, even being in such close proximity. It's like the grandparents are in town and we get the chance to sit down on a Friday night and really talk about some conversations we've heard recently (Thanks, Grampy Taylor!).

Can you point to a particular moment or line of inquiry from one of these interviews that illuminates a core value, in your mind, of the conversation between poets as a form?

Sue Sinclair: It's true that this is a rare opportunity for us and I wasn't surprised to find that the question of how to balance writing and other needs and responsibilities was a theme in many interviews. A lot of energy goes into the getting of the bagel! But even when you and I aren't directly engaged in conversation about poetry, I know that "the bagel" is supported by a taken-for-granted understanding of the value of reading and writing. That what makes sharing bagels something we want to do is partly that we both cherish reading and writing. I find that's the case with a lot of my relationships with writers— we'll talk about everything but writing and feel our common commitment supporting the other talk. I feel that when Souvankham Thammavongsa asks Dionne Brand about her birthday. It's a nine-tenths unseen feeling.

But I don't want the shared commitment to remain submerged indefinitely. I do want Brand to quote the lines she does as she and Thammavongsa move from birthdays to aging ("thank heavens for the earth and the sky all indifferent all unconcerned"). That you can take something for granted is a good thing, it suggests trust. But I'm wary of taking anything for granted indefinitely because of course taking for granted can shift into forgetting about. I find it helpful when readers and writers reveal our shared commitment by showing each other how poetry inflects and inhabits our various backgrounds and biographies (even when that commitment has the form of doubt, even as that commitment takes a multitude of shapes). For me that's the value of a collection like this. It's a public witnessing and exploration of each other's literary commitments. It's the social side of writing, social in the sense of recognizing a shared space and negotiating that space in the explicit company of others.

I should note that although the getting and eating of bagels (or birthday cake or fill-in-the-blank) puts pressure on the time to read and write, they're also obviously related endeavours. We may not all write like Raoul Fernandes whose poems, as Tim Bowling says to him, read "as if they're natural extensions of your day-to-day self," but in my mind reading and writing only matter because they have something to do with the rest of my life, as I've suggested above. So there's tension, but there's also affinity.

Sometimes I get weary of talk about poetry; it starts to feel meaningless when it's in danger of taking over the actual reading and writing of poetry. Promotion demands a lot of extra language around one's poems, in a way that can easily be a distraction from the poems themselves. I sometimes feel among writers a hint of reserve, a trace of reluctance to engage in talk about poetry, and it feels like it's about not wanting to drown the act itself. On the other hand, I get lonely without this kind of talk and perhaps too settled in my poetic ways. Direct address can be a powerful spur. When the moment's right, talk about poetry is utterly challenging, energizing and illuminating.

I haven't addressed your question directly but I think I've written enough that I should pass the ball (the bagel?) back to you. Do you want to say something more specific about the "conversation between poets" as a form? What is special about two poets speaking? What is special about *conversation*? Or I can offer you a different direction: You've mentioned *Where the Words Come From*, for which this collection is a sequel: any thoughts about meaningful differences between the two collections?

Thran: "A public witnessing of and an exploration of each other's literary commitments" is a direct answer to my question regarding the value of a publication such as this. To pick up on this idea, I think that while there are other useful, public ways to announce or address those commitments, there is something unique about the manner in which those commitments are communicated in conversation with one person as opposed to, say, on a panel or a social media platform or in a review or a classroom. Even though one may be aware of an audience somewhere in the distance (hi!), each articulation is carried toward a distinct face, a distinct voice, a distinct mind, a distinct email address and these distinctions give the broader discussions a unique and personal shape, one peculiar to the format.

Take the exchange between Armand Garnet Ruffo and Liz Howard where Ruffo gives his own valid, engaged and querying interpretation of *Infinite Citizen of the Shaking Tent* and talks about "burying" the direct address, "deviating" from direct statement. Howard is then able to acknowledge where she thinks he's right ("My ultimate confession… is a disaster of language as a result of trauma") but is also able to clarify and elaborate: "this… excess is really an attempt to render on the pages what is happening in my mind." She seems to be saying that her purpose was not to deviate from direct statement but to address the effects of such deviations (for example, scientific discourse) and contaminants ("substance issues," "Western ideology") on direct statement.

How great for Ruffo to be able to test his interpretation of her work out on Howard, for Howard to be able to respond, and for all of this to happen in an environment of mutual respect and curiosity that we readers then get to overhear! We don't get the luxury of such a clarification in a review, say, and perhaps as a gesture both to each other as poets and to the nebulous idea of a reader of these interviews in the background, we get a more thorough discussion than we might in a direct, personal conversation where, I think you're right, a kind of reticence or reluctance often occurs.

I like what you're saying about trust between poets and the slippery place where that trust becomes "a taking for granted." I sometimes read into my conversations with writers of poetry a strong desire to communicate the passions and enthusiasms that source the work as opposed to the act or process of writing, an act or process which, you're right, is always at risk of encroachment or flood. I'm thinking in particular of that amazing moment when Brand describes for Thammavongsa the camaraderie of the women listening in on "crucial, private conversations" and physically connecting voices from different countries with plugs and wires. Thammavongsa picks up on this as a fitting moment to end the conversation in that she appears to trust it as a metaphor for Brand's poetic practice. To your point about such moments: "challenging, energizing, illuminating."

To your question about the previous volume: generally, and this is true of both the more veteran writers and the newer contingents, I'd venture that the assumption of a poetic mastery acquired with age feels absent from this volume. Good riddance to that illusion. What we have in its place is an assumed familiarity and intimacy with the desire to make meaningful speech, and a mutual respect grounded in that desire. And while broader issues pertaining to the failure of institutional structures were voiced in the previous volume (see Miriam Waddington's interview with Barbara Nickel, for example), of course they're going to be more meaningfully broached in a volume that does a better job of showcasing the real breadth of people writing poetry in this country.

I've no doubt the "white male paradigm" Elizabeth Bachinsky and Kayla Czaga talk about was a real thing, is a crumbling thing, and that the poets queering and creolizing (thanks to Canisia Lubrin for that new-to-me term) the language are finally being heard (and here I'm talking about their poems as well as other testimonies to lived experiences among dominant social structures). The boldness, energy and urgency being injected into Canadian society is being injected into the poems as well, and there are a lot of fine reading lists on offer in these interviews. I think that this particular volume showcases this energy and that there are fewer where-our-works-square-against-the-Western-Tradition discussions (though the Amanda Jernigan and Karen Solie conversation is as deep and intricate a trip down that well as I have read in interview format). But "the deep onus of imagination," as Russell Thornton eloquently puts it, necessarily extends across traditions and has multiple channels. In interviews like those between Linda Besner and Sue Goyette, or between Sina Queyras and Canisia Lubrin, on display is an exertion to cover all of that difficult terrain between the page, the individual body and the wider culture. I love, for example, how Goyette can fit a brilliant synopsis of her approach to line breaks in with discussions about #MeToo, gender studies and Pina Bausch.

Perhaps I've gone on a book reviewer's tangent here at the expense of conversation. I'm curious, as we're talking about conversation, about the social side of poetry and wonder if you can talk about any of the places in these interviews where, as a writer and thinker, you feel seen? Or, to put it in your own words, you "feel less lonely?"

Sinclair: I like your description of direct address: "each articulation is carried toward a distinct face, a distinct voice, a distinct mind, a distinct email address." Exactly. I've said that this mode of address feels powerful but the paradox is that I'm not directly addressed in these conversations (except by you, here). So how does reading these other conversations make me feel less lonely? Perhaps it's that even being a silent witness makes me feel more socially engaged. It's like I'm in the room, at the table. As witness, I'm party to the call to responsibility that comes of the direct address (powerful even, *pace* Levinas, without the face-to-face). And I feel to some degree answerable. That more than any one moment makes me feel socially engaged, "less lonely." Ben Ladouceur describes a related effect when he talks about writing his poems to "an individual, a single human being." He says, "If I have one person in mind as I write, probably a person near to the heart, I wind up with this blood-lined sort of verisimilitude that others, even strangers, can still find interesting and entertaining." A high-stakes conversation one-on-one may also carry some blood-lined verisimilitude—because of the element of answerability, I'd wager.

Of course there are moments that strike a particular chord with me but I hesitate to name them because who really wants a list of my pet concerns! I will say that I respond to the sense of struggle that animates the book. "I had questions... I didn't know how to ask them, but poetry communicated to me in an urgent, life-saving way," says Marilyn Dumont. "Bewilderment as a poetics and an ethics," quotes Karen Solie from Fanny Howe. "I am super confused about what 'the good' is," says Linda Besner. Me too. I'm aware of the dangers of bewilderment replacing urgently needed action, but action without bewilderment also strikes me as inadequate.

Having said that talk about poetry makes me "feel less lonely," I may have implied that writing poetry is lonely-making, but the poetry Canisia Lubrin describes doesn't seem lonely with its home in "the people, the streets, the non-experts." I find, though, that few people are interested in or have the time to commit to the kinds of poetry that feel fundamental to me. On the other hand, reading and writing poetry is a way of keeping company with others, with the land, with the past. Of course, attempting to keep that company and keep it well is often challenging—at both the level of aesthetics and the level of ethics—so "talk about poetry" makes me aware of those challenges and sustains me in attempting to live up to them.

You referenced the fierce energy and urgency that has flooded Canadian poetry and which is on display in these conversations. This collection responds to the demand for BIPOC voices, and the shifts in power and consequent enriching of the poetic landscape are palpable and invigorating. Katherena Vermette writes about the current interest in Indigenous writing that "there is a certain amount of trendiness these days, something about the reconciliation (trademark® to Canada) that has lent to a surge of attention. But that has nothing to do with us, really." I've since been thinking about that "nothing to do with us." The "us" is a powerful gesture, a centring of reality away from the supposed centre in a place that to me, a settler writer, feels exclusive. The "us" (Vermette and Dumont and possibly their kin?) deliberately turns its back on me—not because it bears me any ill-will but simply because its concern has to be elsewhere. So much for my feeling less lonely! But I'm engaged: I'm powerfully called to the privilege it has been for me to "feel less lonely" in the realm of poetry and elsewhere. It's an accidental effect, but I'm very much drawn into the conversation. And I'm grateful that it's taking place in my view.

For the most part in this book, white people are talking with white people, Indigenous with Indigenous and POC with POC. Perhaps that's helpful in creating relatively safe spaces, a place where an exclusive "us" can be claimed, but I wonder if we poets are ready, in our different ways, to do more talking across colour lines. I hope we soon are.

The last thing I'll say for now also has to do with both answerability and this particular cultural moment. It hurts, but I'm not surprised to find two younger women poets reporting that their sense of community has been damaged by ongoing revelations of sexual misconduct, including assault. I also note that this volume includes signatories and former signatories of the UBC Accountable letter; this feels to me like the elephant in the room. Those who find the letter acutely oppressive may resist or ignore these conversations. I have spoken with strong-minded people on both sides of this debate and I cannot resolve it cleanly for myself. What I do feel with my whole body is that I want the younger poets in my midst to feel that I have their backs. When in doubt, take the part of the most vulnerable. For me, that can't mean wholesale condemnation of everyone who has signed the letter; it can mean opening space for young writers willing to give voice to their experiences and concerns and building more accountability into the structures of which I'm a part.

In the midst of this moral struggle, what can this collection offer? Not a cure-all, that's for sure, but at least what you said, Nick: "an assumed familiarity and intimacy with the desire to make meaningful speech, a mutual respect grounded in that desire." An intergenerational conversation that feels non-hierarchical. This sense of a two-way street was foregrounded for me when Kayla Czaga said (in one of just two interviews that seem to have been face-to-face), "I feel like I gel with Elizabeth on an interpersonal level. But then she is so warm and open and thoughtful in a way that, when I was growing up, when I thought about what writers looked like, serious writers, I didn't picture Elizabeth." My hope is that going forward we can continue to turn toward these less-hierarchical relationships without ignoring the power structures in which they may be embedded. As Linda Besner observes, "much of the literary world is in a nebulous semi-personal, semi-professional zone." That's been our downfall, but I hope that being democratically "warm and open and thought-ful" will help us to find our way to more equitable, responsive structures.

Thran: I first got into poetry out of a desire to shake my language from partici-pating in embedded power structures—at least the obviously capitalist ones (the languages of utility, persuasion, manipulation)—but it's been disheart-ening (and, in hindsight, totally obvious) to see that poetry, and the culture around it, is not immune to the sicknesses, the isms (racism, sexism, ableism) and that personally I wasn't actually building a force field or retreat with my own stanzas. In truth, I've ended up perpetuating or fortifying a lot of these structures: in some of my words, some of my associations, some of my aspira-tions, some of my actions.

But if I continue to believe in poetry as language that shakes, reveals, wakes up, then how can't I be invigorated by the cultural moment? By the work of the new (or newly acknowledged) poets, writers and cultural commentators who are challenging these structures head on, who are building new words on the crumbling edifices?

* * *

Sinclair: So this is our third attempt at having a live conversation. The prob-lem is that it feels very unnatural and it feels pressured in a weird way that is making me very uncomfortable. But we thought we'd give it another shot because…

Thran: Because Ben Ladouceur and Steven Heighton were talking about the more off-the-cuff, unthought—not unthought but…

Sinclair: Unthought-out?

Thran: …unthought-out, more immediate responses and I thought here we could potentially juxtapose those against the longer responses, that there might be a kind of lyricism to that conversation…

Sinclair: In your dreams, Ladouceur! [*Both laugh*]

Thran: …as opposed to the prose of our thoughts recollected in our separate rooms.

Sinclair: So Ben Ladouceur suggested that there was more honesty in speaking out loud, having the words come out of our mouths. I feel like I resist that idea because—I suppose Heighton says this already but—what I say isn't what I think, it's a movement toward what I think and sometimes that's a movement away from what I think and it can be misrepresentative of myself and of whatever it is that I'm trying to talk about.

Thran: Yeah, and I guess that I would agree with that, yet there's still the condition of having to speak with one another. But I think in this context what is removed is a bit of informality and also the disposability of the off-the-cuff remark. I could say something or test something out, but if I misstated or said something that I didn't actually believe or that needed further clarification, I'd have the tools at my disposal—through email, through letter or phone conversation or through just seeing that person again—to clarify or elaborate. Yet this form here that we're doing right now, talking in person for publication, doesn't provide those opportunities.

Sinclair: Well that's the thing. Normally when you're speaking off the cuff it's ephemeral, right? You say it, it's gone and if it's misrepresentative in any way it has disappeared. No one's going to read it. So speaking with an eye to the page is very different from just speaking with an eye to… life.

Thran: So now I'm asking myself if I actually believe that an off-the-cuff remark could be described as disposable in the context of… words-mean-things and things-said-in-person-affect-other-people. Do you think that it is just ephemeral, that it disappears into the air?

Sinclair: No, or it wouldn't be so scary to speak. It's true that words can affect people deeply, but when they're written down there's a further degree of permanence.

* * *

Sinclair: So we've transcribed some ephemera—and have unintentionally demonstrated the point about the desire to refine one's words, to have second thoughts. This seems an apt desire for an afterword: wanting words after words! But perhaps that's enough words for now.

Thran: Then I'll have that last bagel.

CONTRIBUTORS

Elizabeth Bachinsky is a mom, wife, educator and the author of five books of poetry including *Home of Sudden Service, God of Missed Connections* and *The Hottest Summer in Recorded History*, all published by Nightwood Editions. She teaches poetry and creative non-fiction at Douglas College where she is the chair of a wee, but mighty, creative writing department. Her books have been nominated for awards including the Pat Lowther and the Governor General's Awards and her recent creative essay, "Eight Things," was co-winner of the 2018 Kobzar Literary Award. She fled Vancouver in 2013 for a better life in New Westminster, BC. She found one.

PHOTO: DAVID ZILBER

Linda Besner's second poetry collection, *Feel Happier in Nine Seconds* (Coach House Books, 2017), was a finalist for the A.M. Klein Award. Her first book, *The Id Kid* (Signal Editions, 2011) was named among the *National Post*'s Best Poetry Books of the Year. Her poetry has appeared in *The New York Times Magazine* and *The Boston Review,* and her nonfiction has appeared in *The Guardian, The Walrus, The Globe and Mail, enRoute* and aired on CBC Radio. In 2015 she was selected as one of the Writers' Trust of Canada's best emerging artists, and her work has been anthologized in *The Next Wave: 21st Century Canadian Poetry* and *Best Canadian Poetry*. She lives in Montreal.

Tim Bowling was born in Vancouver and raised in the nearby town of Ladner, BC. He now lives in Edmonton, Alberta, and is the author of thirteen poetry collections, five novels and two works of non-fiction. His work has earned him two Governor General's Award nominations, two Canadian Authors Association Awards, two Writers' Trust of Canada nominations, a Plantos-Acorn Peoples' Poetry Award, five Alberta Book Awards, a City of Edmonton Book Prize and a Guggenheim fellowship. His most recent collection is *The Duende of Tetherball* (Nightwood Editions, 2016).

Dionne Brand is a renowned poet, novelist and essayist. She was poet laureate of the city of Toronto from 2009-2012 and is a member of the Order of Canada. Brand's poetry has won the Governor General's Award, the Griffin Poetry Prize, the Trillium Prize for Literature, the Pat Lowther Award and the Toronto Book Award. Her critically acclaimed novel, *What We All Long For*, won the Toronto Book Award. Her latest novel, *Love Enough*, was shortlisted for the Trillium Prize for Literature in 2015. Brand's non-fiction works include *Bread Out of Stone* and *A Map to the Door of No Return*, which has been widely taken up in scholarly work on being in the Black diaspora.

PHOTO: JASON CHOW

Kayla Czaga is the author of *For Your Safety Please Hold On* (Nightwood Editions, 2014), which was nominated for the Governor General's Award, the Dorothy Livesay Poetry Prize, the Debut-litzer and was awarded the Gerald Lampert Memorial Award. She holds a MFA in Creative Writing from UBC. Her second collection, *Dunk Tank*, will be published by House of Anansi in 2019. She probably poured your beer or made your latte at least once.

Marilyn Dumont's first collection, *A Really Good Brown Girl* (Brick Books, 1996), won the 1997 Gerald Lampert Memorial Award. This collection is now in its fifteenth printing and has been reprinted as a Brick Books Classic with a forword by Lee Maracle. Her second collection,  *Green Girl Dreams Mountains* (Oolichan Books, 2001), won the 2001 Stephan G. Stephansson Award from the Writer's Guild of Alberta. Her third collection, *that tongued belonging* (Brick Books, 2007), was awarded the 2007 Anskohk Aboriginal Poetry Book of the Year and the McNally Robinson Aboriginal Book of the Year. *The Pemmican Eaters* (ECW, 2015), her fourth collection, won the 2015 Stephan G. Stephansson Award. Marilyn has been the writer-in-residence at the Edmonton Public Library, the University of Alberta, the University of Toronto-Massey College, Windsor University, Brandon University and Grant MacEwan University. She is an associate professor at the University of Alberta in the Faculties of Arts and Native Studies.

Raoul Fernandes lives and writes in Vancouver with his wife and two sons. His first collection of poems, *Transmitter and Receiver* (Nightwood Editions, 2015), won the Dorothy Livesay Award and the Debut-litzer Award for Poetry in 2016, and was a finalist for the Gerald  Lampert Memorial Award and the Canadian Authors Association Award for Poetry. He has been published in numerous literary journals and anthologies including *The Best of the Best Canadian Poetry in English*.

Sue Goyette lives in Halifax and has published six books of poems and a novel. Her latest collection is *Penelope* (Gaspereau Press, 2017). She's been nominated for several awards including the 2014 Griffin Poetry Prize and the Governor General's Award and has won the CBC Literary Prize for

Poetry, the Bliss Carman, the Pat Lowther, the J.M. Abraham Poetry Awards, the Relit Award and the 2015 Lieutenant Governor of Nova Scotia Masterworks Arts Award for her collection, *Ocean* (Gaspereau Press, 2013). Sue teaches in the Creative Writing Program at Dalhousie University.

Steven Heighton's most recent collection of poems, *The Waking Comes Late* (House of Anansi, 2016), was a Raymond Souster Award finalist and received the 2016 Governor General's Award for Poetry. His 2006 novel, *Afterlands* (Vintage Canada), was cited on "best of year" lists in publications in the US, the UK and Canada, and is now in pre-production for

film. His short fiction and poetry have received four gold National Magazine Awards and have appeared in *London Review of Books, Poetry, Best Canadian Poetry, Best American Poetry, Tin House, TLR, Agni, Zoetrope* and *New England Review*. Heighton also teaches workshops, translates poetry and reviews fiction for the *New York Times Book Review*.

Liz Howard's *Infinite Citizen of the Shaking Tent* (McClelland & Stewart, 2015) won the 2016 Griffin Poetry Prize, the first time the prize has been awarded to a debut collection. Her recent work has appeared in *Poetry Magazine, Camera Austria* and *The Walrus*. She is of mixed European and Anishinaabe descent.

PHOTO: E. ROUSSEAU

Born and raised on Treaty Nine territory in northern Ontario, she is currently the 2018-2019 Canadian writer-in-residence at the University of Calgary.

Amanda Jernigan is the author of three collections of poetry—*Groundwork* (Biblioasis, 2011), *All the Daylight Hours* (Cormorant, 2013) and *Years, Months, and Days* (Biblioasis, 2018)—and of the chapbook *The Temple* (Baseline Press, 2018). Her poems have appeared in journals in Canada and abroad including *Poetry*, *PN Review*, *The Walrus* and *The Nation*; they have also been set to music, most recently by American composer Zachary Wadsworth. She is the editor of *The Essential Richard Outram* (Porcupine's Quill, 2011) and, with Evan Jones, of *Earth and Heaven: An Anthology of Myth Poetry* (Fitzhenry & Whiteside, 2015). She is an essayist, poet and has written for the stage.

PHOTO: JOHN HAMEY

Ben Ladouceur is a writer living in Ottawa, Ontario. His first collection of poems, *Otter* (Coach House Books, 2015), was selected as a best book of 2015 by the *National Post*, nominated for a 2016 Lambda Literary Award and awarded the 2016 Gerald Lampert Memorial Award for best debut poetry collection in Canada. In 2018, he received the Dayne Ogilvie Prize for Emerging LGBT Writers. Ladouceur has published short fiction in such magazines as *Maisonneuve*, *Prism International* and *Prairie Fire*, and his second collection of poems, *Mad Long Emotion*, is forthcoming in 2019, also with Coach House Books. He writes an irregular column for Open Book.

Canisia Lubrin, writer, teacher and editor, was born in Saint Lucia and now lives in Whitby, Ontario. Her reviews, poems, short fiction and non-fiction have appeared in journals and anthologies such as *The Unpublished City*, *Brick*, *Vallum*, *The Globe and Mail* and *Best Canadian Poetry*. Lubrin's debut poetry

collection *Voodoo Hypothesis* (Wolsak and Wynn, 2017), finalist for the Gerald Lampert Award, Pat Lowther Award and Raymond Souster Award, has garnered honours including a CBC Best Poetry Book of 2017.

Sina Queyras is the author of nine books, most recently *My Ariel* (Coach House, 2017). Previous books include *MxT*, winner of the QWF Award for Poetry, the ReLit and the Pat Lowther; *Autobiography of Childhood*, finalist for the Amazon First Novel Award; *Expressway*, nominated for a Governor General's

Award; and *Lemon Hound*, winner of the Pat Lowther and Lambda Award for poetry. She lives in Montreal with her partner and two children.

Armand Garnet Ruffo is a member of the Chapleau (Cree) Fox Lake First Nation with familial roots to the Sagamok (Ojibwe) First Nation. He is the recipient of an Honourary Life Member Award from The League of Canadian Poets and is currently the Queen's National Scholar in Indigenous Literature at Queen's University in Kingston, Ontario. His most recent book of poetry was *The Thunderbird Poems*

PHOTO: PEARL PIRIE

(Harbour Publishing, 2015); a new collection is forthcoming from Wolsak and Wynn in 2019.

Sue Sinclair is the author of five collections of poetry, all of which have won or have been nominated for national and/or regional awards. Her most recent book, *Heaven's Thieves* (Brick Books, 2016), won the 2017 Pat Lowther Award. Sue was inaugural critic-in-residence for CWILA (Canadian Women in the Literary Arts); she has a Ph.D. in philosophy and currently teaches creative writing at the University of New Brunswick.

Karen Solie's fifth book of poetry, *The Caiplie Caves*, will be published in Canada, the US and the UK in 2019. She has taught writing and served as writer-in-residence for universities across Canada and the UK, and is an associate director for the Banff Centre's Writing Studio program. She lives in Toronto.

Souvankham Thammavongsa's fourth poetry book is *Cluster* (McClelland & Stewart, 2019).

PHOTO: ZACHARY PEARSE AT KIEHL'S

Russell Thornton is the author of *The Hundred Lives* (Quattro Books, 2014), shortlisted for the Griffin Poetry Prize, and *Birds, Metals, Stones & Rain* (Harbour Publishing, 2013), shortlisted for the Governor General's Award for Poetry, the Raymond Souster Award and the Dorothy Livesay BC Book Prize. His other titles include *The Fifth Window, A Tunisian Notebook, House Built of Rain* and *The Human Shore*. His newest collection is *The Broken Face* (Harbour Publishing, 2018).

Nick Thran is the author of three collections of poems, two of them—*Earworm* (2011) and *Mayor Snow* (2015)—published with Nightwood Editions. He works as a poetry editor for Brick Books, as a bookseller for Westminster Books and has written about books for *EVENT*, *The Globe and Mail*, *Lemon Hound* and other publications. He lives with his wife and daughter in Fredericton, New Brunswick.

Katherena Vermette is a Métis writer from Treaty One territory, the heart of the Métis nation, Winnipeg, Manitoba. Her first book, *North End Love Songs* (The Muses Company, 2012) won the Governor General's Award for Poetry. Her novel, *The Break* (House of Anansi, 2016), was a national bestseller and won multiple awards including the Amazon.ca First Novel Award. Her picture book series *The Seven Teachings Stories* and graphic novel series *A Girl Called Echo* are both published through HighWater Press (Portage & Main Publications). Her second book of poetry, *river woman*, will be published in 2018 (House of Anansi).

PHOTO: KC ADAMS

Phoebe Wang's debut collection of poetry, *Admission Requirements*, was shortlisted for the 2018 Gerald Lampert and the Pat Lowther Memorial Award. She is the author of two chapbooks, *Occasional Emergencies* and *Hanging Exhibits*, and won the 2015 *Prism International* Poetry Prize. She served as a poet-in-residence with Poetry in Voice and assisted with the curation of *The Unpublished City*, Volumes I and II, anthologies for Toronto-based emerging writers. She is a first-generation Chinese Canadian and lives in Toronto.

PERMISSIONS